Made to Lead

Effective Vedic ways to bring out the leader in you

Col. Karan Kharb

First published 2003

ISBN 81-86685-39-1

Published by
Wisdom Tree
C-209/1, Mayapuri II,
New Delhi 110 064
Ph.: 25130720, 25491437

Printed at
Print Perfect
New Delhi 110 064

Dedicated

to

my mother Smt Kalavati Devi

who fought through and triumphed

over heavy odds in early life!

Adored by all, ignored by none,

she spread love and compassion

for a full hundred years of a multi-coloured life.

She continues to inspire us as we move on...

CONTENTS

ACKNOWLEDGEMENT

This book is the fruition of many people's efforts. I have encroached upon the precious time of Mr Vijay Rao, Managing Director, Vanguard — a lighthouse for high achievers in the corporate world of today. Vijay, a rare blend of social effectiveness and entrepreneurial excellence, has already carved a prestigious niche for himself as a TV anchor and analyst. For this book, I found a great guide and friend in him. I can never thank him enough.

I thank Mr Pramod Prahladka, Vice-President, Motilal Dulichand (Pvt) Ltd, a successful industrialist with a difference — injecting ethical values in business — for his great friendship. Pramod was always forthcoming to spare his valuable time whenever I wanted. His discussions have been a valuable contribution, I'm grateful to him.

In Prof. Lalit Lal, Director, Apeejay Institute of Management and Information Technology, Dwarka, New Delhi, I found a friend who is a gifted scholar, manager and an educationist — all beautifully packed in one! I am grateful for the help and inspiration I received from him.

I am also thankful to Shobit Arya, my publisher — a zealous entrepreneur and successful manager, who has not only been involved in publishing, but has rendered very valuable advice from time to time on the contents and layout of the book. Shobit is young, but many times older than his years in business acumen and maturity — much like a hundred-year old matured wine! Piquant, but delicious! I am indeed grateful, Shobit.

Brig. K. Narendra Singh, a fine blend of Shakespearean thought and Napoleonic verve, has been an outstanding leader not only in the field of soldiery, but also in the corporate world. The perfectionist in him has inspired me for long. I am indebted to him and would continue to draw more from him, for I know there's a lot more hidden in him!

I have also drawn a lot of inspiration from the leadership-in-action of some illustrious Indian military leaders, working with whom was an experience of great learning. My sincere thanks go to Gen. S.S. Mehta, Army Commander, Western Command, Lt Gen. O.S. Lohchab, Director General, Military Intelligence, Brig. K.S. Sharawat, Brig. M.S. Balhara and a host of other friends in academic and corporate fields, and also my colleagues-in-uniform for whose names this limited space is grossly inadequate.

At home, I have been a nuisance to Kamal, my wife, for remaining confined in my study and not giving her time, nor to her maid to clean up the room! I am grateful to her for tolerating me while writing this book. Kamal, I'm sorry, darling; you'll now have a cleaner house — and a more tolerable me too!

Simi and Manu, my daughter and son (Smriti and Varun as others know them), waited for this book to be completed early so that we could all go out for a holiday to Manali. Their tangy observations on my writings often flared up hot debates at home too. I am touched by their tender aspirations and great understanding. Thank you, my children, I carry your debt.

Finally, I am thankful to all those enterprising people who shared their experiences and have enriched my knowledge during my interaction with them, either at the Turning Point India (Noida) or in their companies during in-house workshops.

KARAN KHARB

INTRODUCTION

After expounding on the pain and misery that war brings in its wake, a teacher elicited her students' responses by asking them to comment on the impact of war.

"I hate war!" exclaimed one of the students.

"Why?" asked the teacher.

"Because it makes history!" said the boy, to qualify his reason for detesting war.

How much should we learn? What all can we learn? I empathise with this little schoolboy. With info-explosion today, we seem to have bitten more than we can chew in the field of structured academic learning. Children are overloaded with school bags bursting at the seams; harassed parents appease school teachers and negotiate with money-mints, called tutorials, which have become a very familiar profile of today's society. Everybody seems to be in a mad rush — even though many do not know where to! They are rushing just because others are rushing. Ill-defined directions and unknown destinations! The only thing that is clear and unambiguous in minds today is the *desire to lead*, even if means and directions are wrongly chosen. Frustrations set in faster these days as people feel left behind. You may avoid reading history of wars, but you cannot avoid the virtual battlefield of modern competitive environments. If you ever desired to get ahead, believe me — you are made to lead! Your desire to lead is the fuel — the propellant without which the best of the machines or projectiles would reach nowhere. It is all packed in you. There is a need to explore and awaken your latent powers, focus them and move in the right direction as a leader. Stoking the fire and awakening the leader in you is the primary mission of this book.

Time was when people's life moved at a snail's pace. It used to take a couple of days for the Emperor in Delhi or Agra to hear about an uprising building up against him in regions as close as Lahore or Avadh. The world has come a long way since then. Even until a few decades ago, if you held a graduation degree, you could be sure of a reasonable career. Graduation has now lost its sheen since long. Technocrats thought that now the future would belong to them. This fallacy too crumbled in no time.

What is now being increasingly realised by the world is that structured educational programmes equip you only with *technical skills*. To be *technically* competent in the field of one's activity is, no doubt, a prerequisite to start a profession. But it is not all. In an environment where there is no longer a dearth of technically qualified professionals, the competition is naturally fierce. Today, when you go to the market to buy a cell-phone handset, you tend to compare and select one which is either very cheap, or is provided with many additional facilities, even if it costs a little more. The same is true of hiring people in today's job market. What options do you have? Either be 'cheaply' available or add on additional value to yourself. That's what is being asked today. What *additional* value do you have over others? How are you going to be *more effective* than others as a leader? How do you solve those *problems* that have no answer or solution through your academic formulae? You need to click with times, environment and people in a much more natural and, yet, effective manner today. You, therefore, have to equip yourself with additional skills to handle people and situations more advantageously. How does one achieve these skills?

That precisely is the aim of this book — equip its readers with *sharper* leadership skills in their personal as well as professional life. In fact, when I began writing this book, I intended to give readers their most trusted companion-cum-coach. A lot of in-depth study has gone into the making of this book. It is not a mere compilation of readings and musings from here and there. It is a result of thirty years of man-management experience in a profession where a leader has to motivate and lead people to give not merely their sweat and toil, but their last ounce of blood too. It also contains the essence of what I have learnt through my sustained study of human behaviour — not from a psychological perspective, but from empirical learning. At Turning Point India (Noida), I found many opportunities to interact with corporate groups during my workshops on subjects covered in this book, and on some more. A large number of housewives, executives, teachers, lawyers, doctors, nurses, engineers — a few 20-years old and some even 60-years young — have thronged my institute to either consult or to attend my personality development sessions. I have learnt a lot from them and this book contains the essence of that learning too.

Development of character as also the acquisition of important skills is the crying need of the hour. Transforming our attitudes, exchanging our thoughts and ideas, facing and conquering problems and converting them into opportunities, taking effective decisions and making the best use of the most valuable but ever-depleting resource — Time — can you see anything worthwhile happening in life without arming yourself with these skills? I have attempted to compress these into one book; a book which will give the readers what they need most in today's life moving on fast track.

I have been exposed to Vedic literature since my early days; it has been my prime source for developing inspirational values. Unfortunately, some commentators and translators tend to shroud Vedic teachings in mystery, which deter readers from taking to spiritual learning. In this book, I have tried to describe the relevance of Vedic thoughts in our daily life. I do not claim perfection in my translation of the Vedic *mantras* quoted in this book. My attempt has been to provide the reader a credible source of inspiration and to emphasise the relevance of Vedic teachings in modern life. Vedic literature has a unique peculiarity: it transcends Time and retains its applicability to all times and all facets of human life. Saints and scholars have often differed in their perceptions and explanations of the Vedic content. I have relied more on Swami Dayanand Saraswati's explanations since he has sought to remove the mystery and superstitions from our most valued treasures of knowledge and wisdom. I wish to apologise to my readers for any inadvertent error in my effort. I shall feel deeply indebted for any learned advice and comments that emerge from the readers on this.

How to Use this Book

As I said, it is not a book that you read in one sitting and cast away into the *raddi* (rubbish). It is your companion-cum-coach. Remember to highlight the message or the idea you find that has direct effect on you. Each chapter has a Focus, which you must read repeatedly. Every time you read these points in Focus, it will give birth to new thoughts and ideas in your mind. That's the aim. If it happens to you, congratulate yourself — you are on the right path. Focus is followed by a Specific Action Plan. Sit down at a time and place where there is no disturbance. Attempt the questions given therein in point form. Also, write down your ideas in point form and explain how you wish to carry out the advice/suggestions given therein.

Carry this book always with you. Flip through the pages, skim through the highlighted lines or words, and in no time will the message vibrate in your mind. Write down your fresh ideas in the space available in the Specific Action Plan pages or on a separate diary. After you have read the entire book and made your notes as I have advised, devote an hour weekly in a place of quietude to your book and these notes. I assure you, it will change things in no mean measure!

As a human, you are the finest creation on this planet. God's isn't a profit-oriented enterprise. So, He would neither manufacture nor consign substandard products here. You have it in you. You are MADE TO LEAD! Start now. Here's the way you can do it!

Happy reading, happy journey to success and glory!

Nature's Reminders to Man

Torrents of a thousand mountain-falls
cannot make a single-watt bulb glow,
until tunnelled through a guided path,
to move a turbine for the power to flow!

Clouds of steam drift and dissolve in the sky,
untapped fuels in Earth's womb lie in dust,
but never make a train roll or a plane fly,
until channelled to drive inner pistons first!

Ample gases, solar heat and fuels on Earth,
bloat the space; parch and scorch every corner;
yet, they do not kindle in homes a single hearth,
until refined and funnelled to ignite a burner!

Ever thought of the fierce power of fire?
It can raze towns and forests to rubble and mire,
and yet not cook for us a morsel of food,
until tamed, managed and carefully ruled.

Infinite potential and talent in humans too lie galore.
Yet, no personality ever grows great or truly ripe,
until it is focused, trained, motivated and more—
until you bring in a *turning point* in your life!

— Karan Kharb

Watch your thoughts, they become words.
Watch your words, they become actions.
Watch your actions, they become habits.
Watch your habits, they become character.
Watch your character, for it becomes your destiny.

— Anon

1

THE POWER OF ATTITUDE

The world is not what it seems; it indeed is what we are! Everything in life depends on how we look at it. Have a look at this. On a hot summer afternoon, when you step out of your home or office, you do not wish to swelter in the sun. So, you reach out for your sunglasses. You wear them and suddenly feel more comfortable. The surroundings look greener, prettier and more soothing. The intensity of the glare of the sun seems a great deal less. You experience genuine relief. But has anything in Nature really changed? No, not a wee bit. There is no fall in temperature. You are still under the same sun. Nevertheless, you do experience immense relief and feel the difference so clearly. Yes, there is a change. Your sunglasses have changed your perception of the reality outside the frame. Your view has now changed. And see how good you feel! 'We don't see things as they are; we see things as we are!'

We routinely come across instances where people react to the same situation very differently. Similarity of the situation does not result in similarity of reaction from individuals. When faced with a challenge, a person may feel his spirits sag or heart to break, or even see the end of the world coming. On the contrary, the same situation can trigger an extra amount of zeal and enthusiasm in another person, enabling him to tackle it better. The situation is, therefore, not the source of happiness or sorrow because, if it were, reactions of both the people would be similar.

So, attitudes play a very significant role in our lives. Long ago, there were emperors and affluent merchants who enjoyed the fruits of life in this world, even though they did not have the luxury of electricity, cell-phones, air-conditioners and the virtual array of modern gadgetry. Today, electricity failure for even an hour seems to seriously disrupt the life of the common citizen. Why? Not because electricity has become the prime support to sustain life, but, because our experiences and habits have so changed our *attitudes* that we treat these amenities as indispensable.

RESURRECTING FROM HUMAN WRECKAGE!

As a Captain in the Army, I was posted at the Indian Military Academy, Dehradun. From there, I was called to my Regimental Centre, Danapur (Bihar) to attend the Biennial Conference, in 1981. Casualties of the Indo-Pak war (1971), who had suffered disabilities of a permanent nature, were retained after their medical treatment at the Centre, pending their rehabilitation in civil life. These brave soldiers of my battalion wanted me to join them for tea. While chatting with them, I saw that most of them were very cheerful. I, however, noticed one helpless-looking individual standing aside, glumly. When asked why he looked so unhappy, tears rolled down his cheeks and I discovered that he had lost his left foot in the enemy minefield when my battalion had attacked a well-fortified Pakistani post, Wanjal, in Kashmir. He had been treated under expert medical care and an artificial foot fully adapted to suit his requirements was provided to him.

I held great regard for these gallant warriors and viewed their sacrifices with the deepest sense of gratitude as a soldier and a citizen. But I could not bear the sight of a vanquished Ripudaman Singh, pathetically hanging on to his crutches as a gallant war hero holding his gun. Ironically, his name, translated in English, means 'destroyer of the enemy'. The Indian Army has had many illustrious officers who have not only lived with such disabilities, but, also performed every soldierly duty at par with the fittest. There have been army Commanders who have done their job normally without the help of crutches, despite losing both their feet. I had seen one such officer who would take part in every activity with us at the Academy. But, here was a soldier, who had fought so gallantly in the 1971 war, but had since been crying for a whole decade. He could not be rehabilitated because no public or private establishment would accept such a living corpse, hanging on to his crutches. He was a liability to his kith and kin, and to himself. I could not tolerate this. While I admired his bravery in the war, I despised the pitiable condition and disgraceful conduct of a warrior that disgraced his chivalry. I kicked away his crutches and scolded him for being such a wreckage of soldiery. He fell. There were many who tried to help him, but, I did not allow anyone to help him on to his crutches again.

We had won Wanjal. War had ended. A decade had passed but the real Ripudaman Singh was still lying and crying in the same old vanquished, now largely forgotten, minefield with the tiny shreds of his left foot. The bigger and fuller surviving part of him was without him. The real Ripudaman Singh was dead; the living one was just a poor shadow of someone who once was! My harshness and brash behaviour was not liked by anybody in the group at that time, as was eerily conveyed to me by their deafening silence and stares of disapproval. But, I did my best to rekindle in him the fire he had lost. I told him that whatever was possible in this world was already given to him. Nature's laws were such that there was no chance of his growing his lost foot again, like plants do. I cited the example of those officers who were walking and running with artificial limbs without any tell-tale signs of physical handicap. I told him that losing his foot was a brave act and his sacrifice would be revered by people, only if he exhibited pride and dignity in his deeds as a brave warrior. It was up to him to decide whether he wanted to pass his remaining life as a person to be pitied by others and dumped by his own family as a useless burden or as a war hero, still capable and full of zeal and spirit. I told everyone present that I had come to have tea with brave soldiers who were proud of their wounds and sacrifices; not with cowards who loved to drown in self-pity. And in a huff I left, without having tea!

A year later I got posted to the Centre (Danapur). One day, a neatly attired civilian with smart moustache, confident deportment and perfect gait entered my office. He wished me *Jai Hind* and, handing me a packet of sweets, touched my feet. I was taken aback by the obsequiousness of a person whom I did not even know. When I asked him who he was, he told me that he was the same Ripudaman Singh whom I had reproached a year ago. After I kicked his crutches that day, he had vowed never to use them again. He began using an artificial foot that changed his outlook on life. He soon got a job in a Bank and was well settled within six months of the change in his attitude.

The government and the Army had done their best in treating and rehabilitating Ripudaman Singh. But ten long years he had passed, languishing in self-pity. No amount of 'welfare', 'monetary help' or 'sympathy' worked in restoring him from his helpless existence. I had no power to change him either. But, his encounter with me made him grapple with his attitude. The day he changed his attitude from negative to positive, he found a new taste for pleasure in life. From being a useless burden, Ripudaman Singh became a proud and useful person, not only for himself, but, also for the society and his family. Now he did not need any 'support'. He had regained his lost status as a 'supporter' of his family. And along with it, he had regained his self-esteem too.

Beliefs play an important part in shaping our attitudes. Some beliefs we inherit from our parents and families; others we acquire through education and experience. However, beliefs can evolve and change for good or bad. Positive attitudes, nurtured through inspiration and action, take roots as beliefs in a person. And it is through this power of belief or faith in oneself that marvels in history have been performed by humans. Even Reiki, yoga, hypnotism would end up as exercises in futility if we were not to have faith in them. These practices cure only those who want to be cured. You cannot be cured if you do not want to be cured. It is simple: in life you can do only those things that you want to do. Things will never happen your way unless you first want, and then initiate effort to concretise your ideas through action.

WHAT IS 'ATTITUDE'?

Different behavioural scientists have defined the term 'attitude' in different ways, depending upon their predilections and fields of research. According to Allport, an attitude is 'a mental and neutral state of readiness, organised through experience, exerting a directive or dynamic influence upon the individual's response to all objects and situations with which it is related.'

Definitions by experts are invariably complex and need simplification. There are two other definitions I find easy to understand: 'A relatively enduring organisation of beliefs, feelings and behavioural tendencies towards socially significant objects, groups, events or symbols'; or 'a general feeling or an evaluation — positive or negative — about some person, object or issue'; or, a similar view though differently stated: 'attitudes are evaluative sentiments — favourable or unfavourable — concerning objects, people or events.'

Without possessing an attitude, we would have difficulty in understanding and reacting to events or in making decisions and conducting meaningful social relationships. Sentiments not only influence our behaviour; they also guide our efforts in life. The significance of emotional intelligence is now recognised more or less universally. It is this aspect of human psychology which makes the difference in the levels of success and happiness. Why would you otherwise find people with vast wealth and worldly powers lying prostrate at the feet of a saint who has renounced almost everything in life? Why is it that abundance of wealth and resources at the disposal of a millionaire fail to satisfy him whereas a hermit, who has no wealth or resources, not even a house, seems not only healthier, but also happier? The wonder drug here is none else but attitude! One's attitude (not wealth or worldly power) can make the real difference.

In yoga too, *dhaarana* (attitude) occupies a niche of great importance. As per *Patanjali Yoga Darshan*, *dhaarana* is one of the eight basic elements of yoga (*ashtaanga yoga*) without which you cannot enjoy the full benefits of the latter.

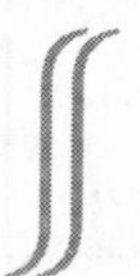

Yama-niyamaasana-pranayama-pratyahara;
dhaarana-dhyana-samadhayo ashtav ni.
— Patanjali Yoga Darshan: 2-29

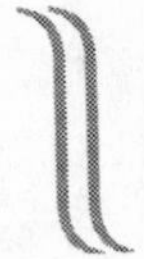

TYPES OF ATTITUDE

Normally, two types of attitudes are of importance for experts concerned with human behaviour — positive and negative. However, a study of the Vedas reveals that there is a third form of attitude too — indifference.

In Vedic philosophy three basic attributes of Nature manifest in humans too. These three attributes are *sattwa*, *rajas* and *tamas* (*satogun*, *rajogun* and *tamogun*). These are present in Nature and the human being is Nature's integral part. The measure of each of these attributes determines the quality of our thoughts and actions. *Sattwa* means 'pure', 'chaste' and 'true'. When we develop this powerful virtue in us, then we are guided by the purest of thoughts and feelings. Besides being noble, our thoughts and actions are positively charged to achieve the desired results.

This is simply so because our desires emerge from *sattwa* and we become so programmed that even unconsciously we entertain only the healthy desires.

Characteristics and Effects of *Satogun*

Characteristics of *satogun* and their general effects on life are as follows:

No	Characteristics	Effects
1.	Truthfulness, honesty and purity	Reinforces trust and loyalty; love and respect.
2.	Compassion	Encourages co-operation and fosters relationships.
3.	Forgiveness	Begets gratitude, concern, love and respect
4.	Patience	Enhances quality of product and efficiency.
5.	Co-operation	Enlists support, dedication, and fosters team spirit.
6.	Sacrifice	Builds effective leadership, motivation and team spirit.
7.	Renunciation	Gives selfless service to organisation, society and humanity.
8.	Poise	Assists in setting high standards through personal examples and confidence.

As a responsible member of the society or an organisation, we champion the good cause for betterment of everyone, including ourselves. We grow with others, not over others! We like to give, rather than take. Our attitude towards life is thus purged of impurities and it becomes positive. The fog clears and we have a clearer vision. Vision, intellect and righteousness are the main driving forces in the individual who acquires the power to see beyond the immediate petty wants. He/she looks for bigger gains for greater contentment in life. Such people do not have to hop from one gain to another. They launch themselves on a success voyage that transcends petty gains and losses to award eternal success, health, happiness and meaning to life.

So, *sattwa* is a force that motivates us with the drive to make us say to ourself: 'I can do a lot for the organisation, society and the world.'

Rajas is an attribute of self-indulgence, luxury and pleasure which one seeks without earning through labour. Such people focus on dreams and lust for 'good' life, but are averse to initiating earnest effort. It can be likened to the many events in our history where kings and rulers remained immersed in their luxury while their subjects starved and suffered in misery. Wherever it happened, dynasties perished. Rome had Nero fiddling when it was burning; India had the pleasure-loving Bahadur Shah 'Rangeela' and his sulking successors who brought to an end the glory of Mughal Empire. When individuals become passive spectators to what they have, they become greedy, inactive and selfish.

Rise in *rajogun* displaces *satogun*, nourishes conceit and ego and drives the individual materially to greed. Spiritual bankruptcy and aversion to nobler pursuits result in clouded vision. Hence, the driving force here is the view: 'The organisation, society and the world can give me a lot more.'

Aa rabhasve maamamritasya
shnushtimachchhidyamaanaa jaradishtirstu te.
Asum ta aayuh punaraa bharaami
rajastamo mop gaa maa pra meshtha.

(O man! Imbibe this positivism (*satogun*) and let this immortalising virtue grow, pervade and prosper all around you. Persevere with your intellect, which I nourish and inspire again and again, to lead a life of virtuous accomplishments. Do not invite misery and suffering by surrendering to indulgence and inaction/indifference (*rajas* and *tamas*).

— Atharva Veda 8/2/1

Characteristics and Effects of *Rajogun*

Characteristics of *rajogun* and their general effects on life are as under:

No	*Characteristics*	*Effects*
1.	Self-indulgence, luxury	Promotes sycophancy; encourages pretentiousness; abhors hard work.
2.	Anger	Damages loyalty and relationships; discourages initiative and creates feeling of insecurity.
3.	Covetousness	Blurs vision; characterised by short-term gains and long-term losses.
4.	Jealousy	Promotes suspicious and disloyal atmosphere.
5.	Back-biting	Promotes internecine wrangles; destroys team spirit; creates suspicion and fear in the atmosphere.
6.	Cruelty	Damages personality; destroys love and respect.
7.	Greed	Promotes disloyalty, intrigues, besides destroying trust and relationships.
8.	Vanity	Boosts arrogance; isolates individual and damages relationships.

Rajogun, if not checked, leads directly to *tamogun*, as if it were a process of degeneration of finer virtues and humanity. People immersed in *tamogun* can be likened to those who are submerged in indolence, passivity and indifference, who lose their conscience and, consequently, the very faith in their own worth as also that of the world. Such people prefer short cuts as they are always in a hurry to accumulate more within the shortest possible time; they indulge in errands which promise more material and carnal satisfaction. Unless corrected midway, success eludes such people in the long run. So does health and happiness in life, despite the huge wealth that one might have amassed. Unlike those driven by *satogun*, 'success' garnered by such people itself turns out to be a hush-hush, lack-lustre affair that is devoid of pleasure and pride of 'achievement'. The driving force is absent and one may be seen whining: 'It is a bad world and luck may be worse. I must grab whenever I can, from wherever I can, and whatever I can with the least effort.'

Characteristics and Effects of Tamogun

Characteristics of *tamogun* and their general effects on life are:

No	*Characteristics*	*Effects*
1.	Laziness, passivity and indifference	Characterised by inaction, these attributes corrode positive qualities and kill one's drive.
2.	Procrastination	The thief of Time, it causes loss of opportunities; one tends to look for excuses to justify inaction or scapegoats to blame.
3.	Indolence	Self-degeneration; gradual loss of intellect, health and self-esteem.
4.	Lust	Pushes you to the lowermost ebb to fulfil your baser desires.
5.	Drowsiness	Impairs sense of judgement, vision and decision-making abilities.
6.	Daydreaming	Helps in creating a fool's paradise, blocks initiative and promotes permissiveness.
7.	Loss of faith in morals	Everything is equally good or bad — nothing really matters; neither honour nor disgrace!
8.	Cursing world and self	Symbolises degeneration; believes in gloom and so attains it too!

Traataaro devaa adhi vochataa no maa no
nidraa eeshat mot jalpih.
Vayam Somasya vishvah priyaasah suveeraaso
vidathamaa vadem.

(Let the enlightened sages guide and inspire us to protect us from sloth, passivity/indifference and anger lest these manifestations of *tamogun* become our masters. Let us be so guided and inspired into such noble (*sattvik*) pursuits that not even our critics may criticise our actions. May we thus become scientifically learned, competent and efficiently steer our lives and lead the world to be worthy of divine love).

— Rig Veda: 8/48/14

POSITIVE ATTITUDE

Positive attitude is the fuel for the engine in you. It grows from *satogun*. It culminates in infinite energy and eagerness to initiate action. You feel healthier and any amount of hard work does not seem to tire you. Admiration and love from others pour in and relationships improve remarkably. Positive attitude is a force that lifts you higher from your present status — social, professional and intellectual. But how do we recognise whether the attitude that we harbour is indeed positive?

Sam chedhyaswaagne pracha vardhayemamuchcha
tishtha mahate saubhaagaaya.
Maa te rishannupasattaro agne bramhaanaste yashasah
santu maanye.

(A positively charged personality, that radiates fire-like brilliance and energy, is driven by knowledge and wisdom, must rise and lead to bring prosperity to the society and glory to himself. Those who will associate and partake in positive initiatives with such a leader too shall attain respect and fame, but not those who are negatively active or indifferently passive/inactive).

— Atharva Veda: 2/6/2

The remarkable fact is that one's attitude cannot remain hidden for long. It manifests itself through our aspirations and endeavours. If a person's attitudes are positive, he /she will be satisfied and will consider himself/herself a success if his/her present status rises to a higher plane. Positive attitude gives greater satisfaction and feelings of self-importance from achievement. Satisfaction does not allow complacency to set in and such people function from a 'win-win' standpoint.

NEGATIVE ATTITUDE

Negative attitude is also a force. It also drives the mind and the body in which it resides. The difference, however, is most significant. While positive attitude takes you on the ascending path, negative attitude pushes you to the lower levels, at times even the baser levels — both in mind and deed. Whenever we slip into negative attitudes, inspiration gets replaced by revenge, admiration by jealousy, co-operation by cunning, goodwill by deceit, zeal by anger and so on.

Maahirbhoorma pridakurnamastaaataanarvaa prehi.
Ghritasya kulyaauparitasya pathyaanu.

(Be positive, co-operative and benevolent; walk not the crooked way like a snake. Also be not negatively active and conceited nor violent like wild animals. Everywhere there is plenty of corn and wealth that you will ever need. Do not be misled by untruth, lust and negativity).

—Yajur Veda: 6/12

It is a self-destructive power that stems from *tamogun*. Persons filled with a negative attitude find it difficult to share others' sorrows and happiness. Such people focus their efforts on their own affairs as they always fear a downward slide and wish to avoid it. Each failure makes them more worried and suspicious. The danger of losing lurks everywhere and they fear most from risk-prone ventures. They always function from a win-lose standpoint. It is strange that they pick up negative lessons from the same situation from which others would pick up positive lessons, e.g. the moral from David and Goliath's story!

Positively-charged people will dispassionately analyse each failure to dig out reasons for the failure and restart after eliminating the shortcomings. The negatively-charged people curse themselves, blame others, their bad luck or even God and switch off. They think failure is the end.

Indifferent Attitude

Positive attitude is an inspirational and enlightening force, while negative attitude is a destructive force. Indifferent attitude is an extinguished force that simmers and smoulders within, without any worthwhile endeavour — positive or negative. People without vision, without ambition, making a living through the humblest and safest means, fall in this category. Such people are bereft of self-esteem and pride. Nothing seems to ignite them. You can neither humiliate them nor arouse them enough.

There are instances where the physically handicapped have performed feats that able-bodied people would shudder to think of. But then there are so many able-bodied beggars in our country who consider themselves worthless and unfit even to earn their own bread. Leave alone beggars, even in affluent families, there are liabilities of similar kind who prefer to live as parasites, without shouldering any responsibility. Such a situation would be ideal for them, if they had the 'authority', but if responsibility must accompany this privilege, then they would rather do without it. These people have neither admiration nor jealousy; neither inspiration nor revenge; neither co-operation nor cunning; neither goodwill nor deceit; neither zeal nor anger— and the unconscious, blissful lethargy pervades their lives. They think they have no control over things in this world. They live because the only other option — death -- is more horrifying. Enjoyment has very limited meaning for them: it is limited to physical comforts, luxury and carnal pleasures.

In positive and negative scenarios, a person has dreams and goals, be they wrong or right. When submerged in an 'indifferent attitude', a person smugly brushes aside all opportunities and adversities without initiating any 'action' to alter the prevailing state. That explains why some brilliantly-profiled people fail, while others, apparently with lesser brilliance, succeed. That is why many a business empire has crumbled, great dynasties have perished over a period of successions marked by 'indifferent attitude'.

Indifferent attitude is more dangerous than negative attitude because it is based on passivity and indolence. It degenerates and putrefies man's very existence.

A person who walks in the wrong direction can be corrected and shown the right path. But, how can a person be shown the correct path who does not want to go anywhere? How can you correct something that does not exist? You can punish a wrong-doer while rewarding a right-doer. But what can you do to somebody who does nothing? Even law does not have provision to punish a person who does neither wrong nor right in the service of his/her parents or society or country.

A delinquent, who hits someone on the road and runs away, can be traced later and charged for his offence and, may be even reformed. Someone who attends to the victim and rushes him/her to the hospital may be rewarded. But can anything be done to indifferent onlookers who crowd around the victim of the accident, but do nothing?

In a fertile land where marijuana or poppies grow, you can sow plants of rose, peas or wheat and these crops will thrive too. But what can you grow in a barren and desolate tract? Indifferent attitude, therefore, needs to be first treated for its primary sterility.

EFFECTS ON PERFORMANCE

Effects of attitudes on our performance were studied by a team of experts. The team conducted the study over 100 executives at different levels in eighteen establishments, ranging from medium to small-scale/cottage and, even, individual entrepreneurs. The survey was conducted on a wide spectrum of executives drawn from manufacturing, trading and service industry. When individual reports on potential, attitudes and future probability of rectitude were provided to the Managing Directors, most of the cases startled them. The individuals themselves, when counselled confidentially, were not only satisfied but also volunteered to undergo a short training programme for self-improvement. The findings were as shown in the histogram given below:

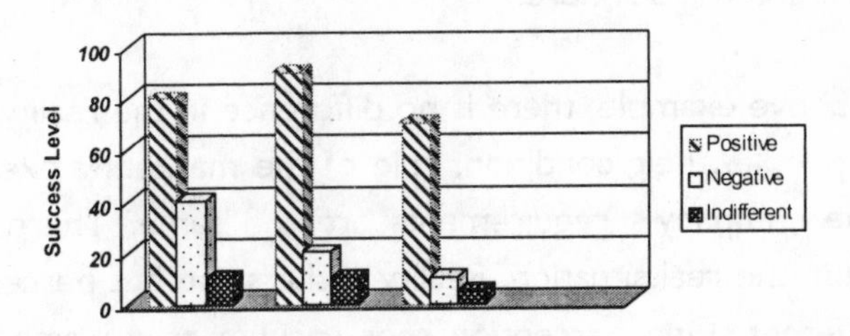

PERCEPTION IS MORE IMPORTANT THAN REALITY!

A fast-growing footwear company had its expansion plans ready. Marketing executives were hired and assigned their territories and targets. One of the executives was assigned a region in central Africa. He and his family celebrated his quick placement in the prestigious company as it came soon after completing his MBA. He flew to the assigned territory but was disappointed on reaching there. He saw people moving around bare-foot, with no footwear shops anywhere. He wondered: 'What kind of society is this? Nobody wears anything on feet here. They have no culture, no sense of footwear. Nothing can sell here.' He cabled back home: 'There is no market for any type of footwear here. Nobody wears shoes or sandals here. You can't sell our product here.' Naturally, he was soon recalled and sacked. Another energetic young executive was assigned the same job. He landed at the same central African town. He also found exactly the same scene. No one wore any footwear. People did not seem to have any idea about footwear, but he was not disappointed. His reaction was in total contrast to what his predecessor had expressed. He was euphoric; not disappointed. He too cabled back home. But his cable read: 'Send a shipload of shoes, sandals — assorted sizes and shapes immediately. No one has any footwear here. It is a huge market. Everything we manufacture will sell here.'

In the above example, there is no difference in the reality. The place, people, their condition, role of the marketing executive and the company's requirements are the same. There is no change in the real situation. Reality is the same but perceptions are different. One perception sees vacuum as a waste space where nothing exists and, therefore, every effort would be futile. The other perception views the same vacuum as a potent space where anything can be sucked in and therefore, a great room (market) for their product. Our achievements are, therefore, a result of how we perceive individual situations. The reality of the situation has lesser relevance in life. That's why we suddenly feel so comfortable under the sweltering sun merely by wearing sunglasses!

Traditions and beliefs, established in Indian society since ages, sometimes make a curious display of how our thinking can influence and control our body and mind. Kumbh is a religious *mela* (fair), which is held once every twelve years during winter, when the mercury often dips to 2 degrees Celsius. In such biting cold, people heat up their rooms and cover themselves with multi-layered woollens. But at Haridwar, people — old, frail and feeble, men and women — unwrap themselves and enter the river to stand waist-deep and pray for hours. Some devotees do so from midnight to daybreak. Compare this with the situation normally seen in city homes — young and able-bodied people catch cold, fall sick due to exposure to cold and rush to doctors.

I have seen people in Moscow removing their clothes, entering ponds and breaking through the frozen crust at -14 degrees Celsius, just for fun! We have not heard of this kind of voluntary exposure killing people, even though we do hear about lots of deaths due to cold waves in towns and villages of India, at times even at higher temperatures. The secret lies in mental conditioning. A strong and tough person becomes vulnerable to much less cold, whereas freezing temperatures fail to unnerve semi-clad people enjoying cold-water dips under sub-zero conditions!

The impact of perception often transcends reason and logic. We have read or heard about the little girl suffering from a terminal disease who thought she was dying while under treatment at the hospital. Through the window by her bedside, she could see the ivy-covered wall of the building, across the road. She witnessed the vine leaves withering day by day. She unconsciously but ominously related her life to the climber and felt that she was weakening increasingly as the vine kept withering day by day. Her imagination led her to gloom and she was soon overwhelmed with the sinister belief that she would die the day the last leaf of the vine dropped. She expressed her worst fears to her boyfriend, who loved her madly and came to visit her daily. The boy was good at painting. The day came when the vine was left with its only leaf at the top edge of the wall. Mary's day passed from despair to momentary spells of relief as she looked at the leaf. The leaf held on as the night fell and so did the girl. Her boyfriend went up and painted the leaf on the wall (in size and colour true to the original) at night, even as the only real leaf fell off. Next morning, the girl woke up and peeped out of the window to see if the end of her life had come. But she found the leaf intact. As days passed, she noticed that the last leaf of the vine held on; her dwindling faith too held on and rejuvenated her lost strength. After a few days, new leaves appeared on the vine, overcoming this girl's worst fears that she would die with the withering of the last leaf on the vine. And lo behold, the girl recovered to survive. The strength that doctors and medicines could not provide came from her own changing perception.

The reality in this case was different and, perhaps, was even corroborated by the medical experts who were sceptical about her recovery from a terminal disease. What was responsible for her recovery? Not doctors, neither relations, nor care; it was her very own perceptions that were shrewdly transformed into a positive influence over her by her boyfriend.

Pauranic Indian literature preaches detachment from worldly allurements because it is a '*mithya maya/mithya sansaar*' (unreal life/unreal world). Everything depends on how we perceive it. Who knows the reality, anyway? Where is God? If we believe He is in us and our thoughts are centred on Him, there is a fair chance of feeling different from those who do not *believe* in God or who believe if He is there, He is up in His Heaven — far away from us. What is the truth? Perceptions shape up different beliefs and our lives are immensely affected by them. If wealth were happiness, no rich person would ever be sad. But we find the rich committing suicide and the poor making merry! Royals can be physically handicapped while the poor are more muscular. Frustrated princes run amuck, destroying their entire dynasty! The underprivileged worker on the road, blessed with meagre resources, rushes to save an unknown life lying prone due to an accident and prays for his survival.

We all have our own notions and understanding of happenings around us. Howsoever conceited and opinionated we may be in our views on life, there does exist a second and even a contrary view. Don't we build our own faith around our own perceptions even when others' viewpoints are at variance with ours? Appreciation of others' viewpoints, howsoever harsh, sometimes work like a scrubbing brush that scrubs the grime off our minds, or like a burning furnace that helps us to reshape and sharpen our blunted edges and points. It can serve as a catalyst in our growth. It is, therefore, more advantageous to be flexible in life and share our viewpoints with others. Differences in ideas actually constitute the basis of all human progress.

Imagine the world without thinkers, philosophers and scientists who questioned the age-old established notions of mankind from time to time. We would be nomads of the primitive type, hardly distinguishable from monkeys. Because of suppression of differences in opinions, societies under dictatorial regimes do not progress as rapidly as open societies. We can never learn anything from henchmen. The key to our learning is through a variety of ideas and opinions. How else could humanity multiply ideas to build wisdom?

A learned father explained this point to his inquisitive son as: "If I have a coin and you have a coin, and we exchange the coins, how many do each of us possess?"
"Obviously, one each."
"And if I have an idea and you have an idea, and we exchange them. How many ideas do each of us possess?"
"Yeah, now we do have *two* each!"

That's the profit and power of sharing our viewpoints, of keeping our perceptions flexible and accommodative. More often than not, our vision is blurred by the very opacity of our fixed views. The picture below shows how perceptions rule our lives. One perception can obliterate the existence of the other in varying degrees. The more strongly we are attached to our own viewpoint, the more difficult it becomes for us to comprehend the other's viewpoint. See the figure below:

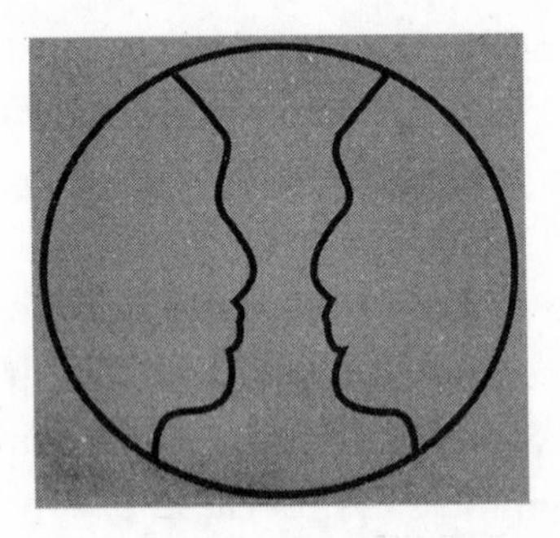

What is it? If you have made up your mind about it, pass it on to your friend and ask him what it is. Do you both disagree with each other? Okay; but who is right? If your first impression gives you the picture of a wineglass, you will most probably bet that the picture is nothing but a wineglass. If your friend laughs at your imagination and shows you two human faces, you are most likely to be amused at his inability to see the wineglass you so easily grasped. But then have another closer look and re-examine. Do you find the picture as seen by your friend? Is it indeed a wineglass or are there two human faces, close enough to kiss each other? Likewise, if you highlight the wineglass picture, your friend may see your perception too.

The picture has not changed. It is a drawing with two shades —

black and white. But your view has changed. Can you now tell who is right and who is wrong? There will be situations in real life too where two opinions, apparently in sharp contrast to each other, can be both right and irrefutably correct at the same time as this figure is. It is important to see and face the situation in its right perspective and respond to it in an appropriate manner after examining its different facets and importance to us, vis-à-vis its relevance to our goal in life.

Correct understanding of the situation is possible only when we keep an open mind. An open mind accepts the existence of a viewpoint different from ours, even if it were twice removed from our own viewpoint. Our findings and solutions will be more objective after such an analysis with an open mind. When we are subjective and self-centred, we create opacity and the other's viewpoint gets lost from our sight. But the moment the other viewpoint becomes apparent to us, the impact on our attitude too gets enormous. The following illustrations explain this reality.

Frank Koch in *Proceedings*, the magazine of the US Naval Institute, once described an incident, which explains how the paradigm shift affects our thinking process to instantly bring in a dramatic change in our behaviour.

Two battleships assigned to the training squadron had been at sea on manoeuvres in inclement weather, for several days. I was serving on the lead battleship and was on watch at the bridge as night fell. Due to poor visibility on account of fog, the Captain remained on the bridge, keeping an eye on all activities.

Shortly after dark, the lookout on the wing of the bridge

reported, “Light bearing on the starboard bow.”

“Is it steady or moving astern?” the Captain called out.

Lookout replied, “Steady, Captain”, which meant, we were on a dangerous collision course with that ship.

The Captain then called to the signalman, “Signal that ship: we are on the collision course; advise you to change course by 20 degrees.”

Back came the signal, “Advisable for you to change course 20 degrees.”

The Captain said, “Send; I'm the Captain. Change course 20 degrees.”

“I'm the seaman, second class,” came the reply. “You had better change course 20 degrees.”

By that time, the Captain had become furious. He spat out, “Send, I'm a battleship. Change course 20 degrees.”

Back came the flashing light, “I'm a lighthouse.”

We changed our course!

The situation remained the same. The ship, the sea, the night, the fog was the same. So were the lights, the lookout and the signalman. But the Captain's thinking underwent a sea change and his decision took a somersault. Why? Because he could see the same situation from another angle. This resulted in the paradigm shift. Once this happens, it brings instantaneous realisation and relief. Frequent realisations of this nature leave an imprint on us and we get accustomed to look for the other's view, which, if available, enables us to take sound decisions. Here was a reality that was clouded by the Captain's initial perception. So often in life, we ourselves experience this happening to us. Reality is often blurred by our subjective leanings and mental fixations.

Strong likes and dislikes or biases and prejudices are often talked about as personal attributes. Some even boast of their stern stand against certain people — not ideas (*sic*). Sometimes we come to dislike certain people or situations without quite knowing why it is so. It becomes difficult for us to justify our stand, but still we do not find it easy to abandon our declared position. I was once addressing a group of regional managers of a multinational insurance company in New Delhi. A decision of the management in a case study was being debated. Some in the audience said the decision was wrong and uncalled for. When the entire case was discussed at length, and the circumstances under which the controversial decision was taken became clearer, most of them agreed that the decision was right and necessary. One of these very senior managers, however, stuck to his earlier stated view: the decision was wrong and uncalled for. When confronted with the fresh inputs and detailed analyses of the circumstances, he did agree that there were compelling reasons for the ultimate good of the organisation that drove them to take the controversial decision. He insisted, "Still the decision was wrong and uncalled for."

I asked him: "Why do you say so even now?"

His response was: "Because, I like to stick to whatever I have said once."

"Even after you have yourself analysed the circumstances and are convinced about the necessity of such a decision…?"

"Yes; because I am a man of conviction and would not like to abandon my declared position. It is purely on moral grounds; not on the merits of the case study…"

Fantastic! Isn't it? But it is more fanatic than fantastic to nurture such chaos in one's mind and lose sight of what is at hand. It is like selling butter to a customer who wants a razor! We have such dogmatists in organisations, families and societies who like to suppress reason under their sheer weight, whenever they fail to muster logic on their side. Such rigidity prevents us from examining situations in a fair manner. This way we do not resolve dilemmas because we tend to bulldoze and crush, despite knowing well enough how destructive our stand might be for us as well as for others. Given the power, such people can be dangerous managers, ruthless officers, tyrant dictators and mad hijackers to spell gloom of the September 11 (World Trade Center) magnitude. A mind closed to reason is indeed dangerous!

Dilemma gives rise to conflict, as it becomes expedient to choose and exercise an option. In such a scenario, exercising an option becomes difficult. What does one do in such a situation? Ask yourself, *'Can I change it? Can I influence it? Can I tolerate it?'* Depending on your answer, you will need to decide on what action to take. If you cannot change it, or directly influence it, can you avoid it? If you cannot avoid it, can you change your view to make it more acceptable?

For instance, if an over-speeding van overtakes you on a busy road, denting your car a bit, would your opinion change if you knew that the driver was on his way to a hospital with a serious patient in it? Or if you saw a man with rowdy children in a quiet restaurant, would you feel empathetic with him if you knew that their mother/his wife had died that morning?

COGNITIVE DISSONANCE THEORY

We come across situations in life when a person behaves in a particular manner, much against his wishes. Likewise, there are also circumstances in which one finds it difficult to behave in the manner one wants to. In both situations, he/she feels dissatisfied and gradually gets drawn into the vortex of inner conflicts. An eligible boy who loves and respects his parents may find it difficult to say 'no' to their suggestion of marrying the girl of their choice, although he does not like the girl. A famous cricket player was under pressure not to confess his receiving huge amounts of money for match-fixing. He did not confess initially but felt so tormented that he could not withhold it, and ultimately confessed. There are innumerable cases in our daily life where we feel one thing but act quite the contrary. This lack of consistency in our attitude and behaviour sets off inner conflicts, though we do so to avoid discomfort. Every recurrence of divergence in our attitude and behaviour causes tension, affecting our personality in a powerful manner.

Harmony of attitude and behaviour can resolve these conflicts. Wherever exists harmony there reigns peace, energy, zeal and contentment. It is thus obvious that one can resolve any conflict in more ways than one.

Leon Festinger propounded in 1957 the *Cognitive Dissonance Theory* to elucidate this phenomenon. It explains the link between 'attitude' and 'behaviour'. Inconsistency or incompatibility between two or more attitudes creates discomfort and the individual tries to reduce it. Festinger thus highlighted belief as a central component of every attitude. In essence, he theorised that cognitive dissonance has the following components:

- It is a state of psychological tension.
- It is generated when a person has two or more cognitions that are inconsistent or do not fit together, e.g. the state through which we pass on running away from the site of the accident in which our car had knocked down a pedestrian. We pray for survival of the victim but do not have the courage to take him to the hospital, or to acknowledge that, as a law-abiding citizen, it is our responsibility to report the matter to the police and surrender, or take precautions and wipe out all tell-tale evidence of the happening. We are sure to be tormented in the latter case.
- It is based on the fact that we seek harmony in our attitudes, beliefs and behaviour and try to reduce tension arising from inconsistency between them.
- We try to reduce dissonance by changing our cognitions about one or more of them.
- It assumes that we will reduce dissonance by looking for additional evidence or by derogating the source of one of our cognitions.
- It asserts that the greater the dissonance, the more we'll try to reduce it.

VALUES, ATTITUDES AND BEHAVIOUR

Relevance of values in influencing our attitudes and behaviour cannot be ignored. Values have varying bearing and significance on individual attitudes and behaviour. We know how people talk about the same set of values, giving totally different interpretations to them to justify their choice of a particular pattern of behaviour. Besides, relative importance of values may also notably vary from person to person or culture to culture.

Some behavioural scientists also noted that conflicts are more easily resolved if we modify our value system. That is perhaps why we sometimes find people generating or acquiescing to a behaviour they were initially opposed to — the police apprehends a culprit but later sets him free due to political pressure, or a teacher defends his favourite student caught copying, or a businessman known for scrupulous living seeks the chartered accountant's assistance to fudge his income-tax returns. Such behaviour is a result of modified value system.

Extensive research by an Australian researcher from Flinders University (Feather, 1991) advocates that values have the following properties:

- They are general beliefs about desirable behaviour and goals.
- Unlike wants and needs, they are either good or bad and have the quality of 'doughtiness' about them.
- They deeply influence and transcend attitudes.
- They provide standards for evaluating actions, justifying opinions and conduct, planning behaviour, deciding between different alternatives, engaging in social influence and presenting ourselves to others.

- They are organised into hierarchies for any given person and their relative importance may vary over a period of time.
- Value systems vary across individuals, groups and cultures.

For managers concerned with controlling and guiding people, the relevance of values is even more significant. Since people's thinking and attitudes can be influenced, it is essential to understand and utilise the properties of these vital forces in influencing the behaviour of the employees, so as to optimise productivity and draw nearer to excellence.

Benefits of understanding attitudes of employees that accrue to organisations are as follows:

- Managers can use their knowledge of his employee's values in order to determine if the dominant values are similar to those held by the organisation.
- An employee's performance and satisfaction are likely to be higher if their values fit well with those of the organisation.
- Selection is the key to ensuring that an individual's values are compatible with those of the organisation.
- Managers can use their knowledge of employees' attitudes, because attitudes influence behaviour.
- Managers can attempt to act in ways that generate positive job attitudes.
- Employers will try to reduce cognitive dissonance in activities that appear inconsistent or are at odds with the employee's attitude.
- Dissonance can be minimised when the employee perceives that it is externally imposed or is beyond his/her control or if any reward can be significant enough to offset the dissonance.

HOW TO IMBIBE POSITIVE ATTITUDE!

Yo jagar tam u samani yanti.

(To him, who is wide awake (discerning and positive), does the applause come).

— Rig Veda: 5/44/14

Ripudaman Singh's story corroborates that attitudes can change and changed attitudes can significantly change the course of our lives. Years of misery just vanish in a moment if we change our attitude. Suppressed energy, lying latent within us and rendered inactive by wrong attitudes, is aroused to give us all we want from it. Vedic philosophy enlightens us about our unlimited potential. *What lies before us and what lies beyond us is tiny when compared to what lies within us* Therefore, we need to explore our inner world. We have to take stock of our lifestyle through introspection in all earnestness.

Consider and ponder over these questions: Are you the Captain of your destiny or is your ship adrift in the sea of life? Have you carefully charted your course or are you aimlessly drifting? No wind can help the ship that is bound for nowhere. Anyone who feels that there is no course correction required in the voyage of life, runs the serious risk of colliding with the lighthouse, as Stephen R. Covey warns in his famous work, *The Seven Habits of Highly Effective People*. Just as undergarments need regular washing, our inner self too needs more cleansing from time to time to reinforce our positive attitude. We need to weed out the negatives and nourish our mental health and energy.

CULTIVATE A P^3 PERSONALITY

Mansoor, a jovial friend but a serious thinker, recently came to India after spending over ten years in Texas. He narrated one of his experiences to me in Delhi. Although the experience itself is simple and we pass through similar situations, few of us take note of the milestones on the highway of life. Mansoor's narration has a lesson for everyone, particularly for those of us who are too overburdened in life. His experience as narrated by him:

I was recently standing in a queue. Isn't that the national pastime this time of the year? Anyway, I noticed that we have become so resigned to Fate that even though there were several people at the desks and most of them were doing their best, there wasn't a smile in the area. Not on those doing the service; not on those waiting in queue.

So, I decided to start humming.

This attracted a few weird looks. I wasn't doing it very loud; just spreading a joyful noise and smiling like I knew something no one else knew... but which I did. The person next to me smiled and nodded at me, so did the person two people up in line. As a matter of fact, it seemed as though everyone standing around became brighter and a bit happier.

Now this could have only been my imagination (it's pretty active) or it could have been that in less than a minute, I changed my attitude, which made the whole situation seem different. This was magic! It seemed to make the queue move faster and I was now making people smile.

My point to all this is, why are we letting a situation determine our attitude? Why is it that we put up with humourless queues, rude people, long waits and endless seriousness when we could be imparting a little more grace, happiness and joy into even the tiniest of our daily tasks?

Mansoor is a *perpetually positive person* (P^3) who enlivens and controls the worst of situations and never succumbs to adversity. Fortunately, there are numerous such persons in the society around us who bring cheer, wherever they go. But then there are also those people who lock out cheer wherever they are. Let's keep out of the latter category, if we want good health, effective professional and social relationships and genuine happiness in life.

Preta jayata nara ugra vah santu bahavah.
(Advance, launch your positive actions and you shall be victorious. Thus, your arms become invincible and illustrious).

— Atharva Veda: 3/19/7

USHER IN THE CHANGE NOW

The day every person in the world acquires a P^3 personality, it would be the dawn of a golden era on Earth. But that would be a utopian view and cynicism would compel even the prudent thinker to think that such an age would never be! Why? Because 'positive' attributes are like crops and fruit-bearing plants, which do not grow indiscriminately like weeds. We never sow weeds and still we find they are a nuisance and overpower the plants we desire to see thriving in our fields and gardens. No manure or insecticide is required for weeds to thrive.

Large tracts in Africa are covered with virgin forests but people still suffer from malnutrition and starve to death for want of foodgrains. We do not find forests that abound in fruit, corn, wheat, paddy or pulses. It is perhaps a less understood law of Nature that useful things do not grow uncared for. Order and discipline is needed for anything good to happen.

Effort, therefore, is necessary to usher in a good life. But once you experience your first paradigm shift, things suddenly become simple and the change receives a positive boost. Things that used to look too formidable earlier become easy for us to comprehend and accomplish.

PRACTISE TOLERANCE

Tolerance is an effortless virtue that conserves energy and exalts us to a higher level of esteem and reputation in public mind. It is a powerful tool which silently influences and gradually places even difficult people at our command. There are innumerable maxims and wise sayings that have been at humanity's service. Some of these are:

- Tolerance is the attitude of Nature, an essence of bliss and tranquillity.
- It forms the best behaviour and it is the form of best behaviour.
- It characterises the cream of society and is the cream of social character.
- It generates glory and glorifies those who generate it.
- It is a lovely lead that leads to love.
- It matters most in most matters.
- It is a great rectitude that returns with gratitude.
- It is the seventh sense that sobers the other six senses.
- It is a vital virtue and virtuous vitality.
- It removes both: the differences and the indifferences.

WEAR YOUR SMILE

Wash off all your negative thoughts and feelings early in the morning with your bath. What do you wear first after your shower when dressing up? Now onwards wear your cheerful smile first. Even when you are alone, you must wear a smile. An expert in skin care and cosmetics suggested that a person earns his/her face from the moods he/she keeps. Your facial lines, your resting demeanour, what your age is — all rest on how you think and behave. If you keep a smile or even a slight grin going, you will age more slowly and gracefully and have a lot more friends; and fewer wrinkles at that!

The power of a smile is so under-rated that some of us feel it compromises our position in authority. Far from being so; your cheer will refill your employees' confidence, zeal and motivate them to a spirited performance. Remember: when you smile, everyone around you joins you; but when you cry, you cry alone—others run away. So now is the time to turn up the corners of your lips!

INCULCATE CONSTRUCTIVE THOUGHTS

The challenge posed by the high speed of modern life is that we are bombarded daily with negative messages — unstable market trends, tougher and newer competitions, heightened insecurity in view of corruption at high places and terror in streets, war clouds gathering on borders and so on. Just refuse to give in. Think of the positive and constructive aspects of every situation at hand. The more you practise, the more easily will it come to you. You are not in control of other people, but you are in control of the most significant thing that matters; and that is your own thoughts. Keep them constructive and positive and you will change every situation you are in. It is not as difficult as some people might think. It is the easiest thing, particularly when you know that other options are much worse, costlier and more risky.

Tan mei manah shiva-sankalpam astu.

(May my mind be full of good intentions and constructive thoughts).

—Yajur Veda: 34/1

SAY 'PLEASE', 'THANK-YOU' AND 'SORRY'

Everyone expects courtesy, love and dignity; and rightly so, I guess! If we could only communicate in a little nicer way and were a bit more grateful, the world would be a much better place to conduct business in. Charity begins at home. But we tend to take everything for granted in our relations — from home to friends to workers to customers. And when their feelings, pressed because of our persistent behaviour, boomerang one day, we do not realise that we ourselves were the root cause of it. So often we fail to adopt the niceties at home. Nicety is never too much. Although one does not demand concern and courtesy, but one does expect it. If someone gave you first-aid and took you to the hospital from the accident site, you will never be able to thank him enough for it.

We must start the ideal behaviour from home. Parents are role models for the growing child, who inherits and copies his parents' behaviour. It is, therefore, essential to do our best, to be kind at heart, cheerful and concerned in our talk and sincere in our actions towards our spouse, children, friends and neighbours. The three words of English language: 'please,' 'thank you' and 'sorry', if loaded with appropriate feelings, play an important role in keeping us happy besides helping to build, consolidate and protect relationships. Only petty people find it difficult to use the expressions listed.

Add Value to your 'Intellectual Capital'

Intellectual capital is a strange phenomenon; it is not always an *asset*. It can be the single most dangerous *liability* too. It is an invaluable asset if supported by positive attitude but becomes a serious liability if it rests on negative attitude. It is like nuclear power, which can be used to annihilate civilisations and wipe out life from this planet. An alternative use of its immense potential is for eradicating human suffering and poverty by harnessing the power for positive ends. That too depends on the 'attitudes' of scientists, politicians and military leaders at the helm. When learning is restricted to mind alone, it is merely 'knowledge' or 'skill' with limited field of use. But when learning involves both mind and heart, it becomes 'wisdom' capable of unlimited use and versatility. When skills are integrated in achieving organisational goals with full commitment and involvement, value is added to *intellectual capital* at work.

Avoid Criticism

There is nobody in a civilised society who embodies only negative attitudes. The worst of us has some positives lying dormant in some inner corner, waiting to be stirred and enlivened. However, if there be such a person who claims perfection and says he/she needs no further self-improvement, he/she needs it most! There is a definite need and scope for every human being to rise a little higher from the present level — howsoever 'high' it may be. Look for only the strengths in your employees, friends and neighbours. Avail of their strengths in business and relations. If you ignore their negatives and acknowledge their positives, you will find that gradually their positives multiply and negatives diminish. Criticism provokes reaction and one tends to defend oneself against accusations. It is a plain fact that though we might be aware of our shortcomings, we do not like others to focus their spotlight on us. Search for something good in others and praise them, for it not only encourages them, but brings us even greater returns — it transforms our thinking to good effect, internal as well as external.

If we were to adopt a bit of these minor points in our daily life, we will soon usher in a great change within us and experience a fresh bloom of a new spring in our life.

BE MAGNANIMOUS

Our character, personality and behaviour are our priceless jewels. Reveal and display these jewels so that their lustre and shine reach out to the outside world too. Make it a personal habit to find — and try hard to find — at least one quality you would genuinely admire in the person you so far hated most. If there is no person whom you ever hated, indeed, it is wonderful. Give a pat to yourself for your magnanimity. But, if someone does come to your mind and you still think he/she does not deserve your appreciation, kindness and love, then you need to sit down and force yourself to find at least one positive quality in that person. If you honestly try, you will find more than one quality in him/her, worthy of your admiration.

If you are a senior executive and have reprimanded or sacked someone summarily, find time to relax and think over it. Ponder, if you took the action purely on the merits of the case or was there a speck of vendetta, hatred or malice at heart. If so, think how best you can repair the damage done and also consider ways to ward off such a recurrence in future. If you were to accept your mistake and assuage the hurt of the subordinate by expressing genuine kindness, your stature as a leader will receive a boost. To err is human; but to repair is divine!

BEFRIEND NATURE

Whenever you are upset, disturbed or tired, do some introspection. It is not anything unusual you are going through. When feeling agitated, stop talking or doing whatever you are doing and retire to your room to seek solitude for a little while. Force yourself to relax. Have a glass of water and concentrate on your breathing. Even in the face of severe stress, keep cool for it will help you to feel better, both organisationally and individually, because it is a dose straight from within. Just imagine the peace and health returning and recharging your body and mind.

Find time to harmonise with Nature by:

- Spending time in watching birds and listening to their chirping.
- Watching the serene sky and space above at night and examining the stars.
- Going out for a picnic occasionally: watching crops, plants in the fields/forests, away from town.
- Watching wildlife.
- Listening to the tranquillity of night under the full expanse of the sky above, away from the hustle and bustle of life, once in a while.
- Starting your day by listening to soft music of your choice.

ATTITUDES: KEY TO HEALTH, HAPPINESS & LONGEVITY

Bhutyayee jaagaranam abhutyayee swapanam

(To be awake and positive is conducive to prosperity, health and happiness; to be indolent is destitution, suffering and wretchedness).

—Yajur Veda: 30/17

Being positive does a whole lot of good to all. More importantly, it does a whole lot of good to you. Being positive helps improve your health, checks wrinkles, stops ageing and restores youthful lustre and glow on your face. It has also been medically confirmed that positive and cheerful people are much less prone to suffer from serious afflictions as hypertension, diabetes, brain tumour, peptic ulcer, asthma, etc. besides a host of other ailments; even senility. It is also a proven fact that happier people live longer.

A friend of mine is a doctor who specialises in kidney transplants. He keeps touring various countries to address health care seminars. He narrated some interesting findings in the field of health. He gave me some research literature. Some of the findings by experts on human attitudes and physical health were incredibly revealing. It has now been established that good health and long life are remarkably dependent upon mental conditioning and attitudes. They confirm that attitudes cause emotional reactions, which strongly affect our immune system, circulatory system and even determine our proneness to accidents. The strength of this correlation between attitudes and health has been perilously neglected by doctors as well as our health education system. Though doctors do acknowledge this correlation, it is grossly underestimated, however.

In 1973, Dr Grossarth Maticek gave a brief test to measure habitual feelings of pleasure and well-being to thousands of elderly residents of Heidelberg, Germany. Twenty-one years later, in 1994 he compared the test scores with health status of the subjects. The results were amazing: the 300 people who had scored highest turned out to be *thirty times* more likely to be alive and healthier than the 200 lowest scorers!

The practical implications of this experiment are highly impressive! Though the test focused only on mental factors, it predicted future health more effectively than much longer tests on traditional risk factors, such as genetics, lifestyle, smoking, alcohol and diet. This means that improving your attitudes can make a greater difference to your health than, for example, quitting smoking or losing weight. Of course, this is not to suggest that you should neglect the risk factors. But imagine the quality of life if you were to enjoy it with a positive attitude rather than the transient pleasures derived from injurious drugs and personal habits.

Though the idea of improving the health prospects by changing attitudes may initially sound like trying to excel in singing through body massage, experiments show that a small amount of training spread over a year can provide astonishingly positive effects. In 1973, Dr Grossarth Maticek conducted yet another amazing experiment which proved just that. He randomly divided 1,200 people who had scored poorly on his tests into two equal-sized groups. One group of 600 was given a self-help brochure and six training sessions of one-hour long, and each spread over a year. The other 600 were given no training. When the health status of the two groups was checked thirteen years later, 409 of the people given the training were still alive with satisfactory to a good state of health. Of the other equal-sized group, only ninety-seven were found living, with the rest having kicked the bucket by then!

If you think it's too late for you to change, think again: the average age of people in the experiment was fifty-eight! It is never late; not even at ninety, to change and add lustre to life.

Focus I: Have a New View to Have a New You!

Acquiring the Right Attitude!

- Get your focus right. You will get what you *look for* !
- You normally get only what you deserve, including criticism, pain and hostile environment. You may require a change immediately to deserve better!
- Imbibe magnanimity. An attitude of gratitude begets you more than you give!
- Your organisation, society and family have a right on you and you have a duty towards them before you expect any returns.
- Follow a healthy and regular programme of self-education and self- inspection.
- Guard against negative influences: friends/associations, literature, media/internet. Remember: pulling down is easier and faster than pulling up — look who's where!
- Love what you do and do only what you love. The result will be a marvel!
- Preserve dignity of your juniors, colleagues and seniors. Praise and guidance achieve better results than punishments and criticism.
- Stop and look within occasionally. Question yourself: *What can I correct in myself to be better and more effective*?
- If others find faults in your actions/behaviour but you don't, it means that they know one less! Get down to it right now!

SPECIFIC ACTION PLAN

A- Lock yourself up in your room and tell others not to disturb you for at least thirty minutes. Look at the mirror on the wall. Yeah, the person looking at you from this mirror is the most sincere friend you will ever find in this world! Together now, 'you + your real self', visualise the value of your vital personality reinforced with vital resources given in the Specific Action Plan. *(Do this exercise daily for at least next thirty days. Make appropriate notes that come to your mind for more specific areas within you that require improvement. Nourish your growth daily by appreciating the change).*

B - Maybe for years you have been planning to 'do something or start something one day'. The time has come; start it right now.

C - You must usher in at least one CHANGE within you. Start with a change in your personal habits. Then determine the other changes you want to introduce in your behaviour/ working style and list them out here and now:

a) Immediate changes

____

____

____

____

____

____

b) Long-term changes

____

____

____

C - When you imbibe these changes, what benefits will accrue to you? Visualise and enumerate the likely benefits:

D- Assign yourself a target, including time stipulation by which to imbibe your intended changes. Then commit yourself to your decision.

E- Make suitable pocket cards or take a notebook and write down the guidelines and your own notes for self-advancement.

To listen well is as powerful a means of influence as to talk well, and is as essential to all true conversation. Listening to a wise man across the table is worth a month's study of books.

— A Chinese proverb

2

Listen, to Make Others Listen to You!

Interpersonal dynamics are a powerful force. All kinds of human interactions and relations are based on skills of communication. On certain occasions, when we find ourselves interacting with multifarious cultural, social and professional groups and individuals globally cutting across races, religions and regions, the import of this powerful human faculty gets even more heightened. So powerful and productive can this skill be that even in the past, statesmen and diplomats endowed with it, have often been the harbingers of peace and prosperity among communities and countries. Their failure in establishing effective communication has been too often — perhaps always — the cause of interpersonal conflicts and even devastations that mankind has suffered through the ages.

Therefore, consequential bottom-line functions like leadership, face-to-face communication and public speaking, mentoring, coaching and mediation/negotiations — all presuppose effective communication. It is this skill that places man in command of the planet. It is this skill through which he expresses his creativity, intellect and emotions. In today's enlightened environment, technological advancement has simplified international communication by placing assorted gadgetry, cell-phones and Internet at our disposal. You can now search or publicise; sell or buy; learn or teach; hire or fire anytime, anyone, anywhere in the world! The stakes therefore on what you say and how you say are much higher since the assortment of media and speed with which the word spreads renders the communication once made irretrievable.

Literature on research conducted in the field of communication reveals that more than 75 per cent of an executive's time in an entrepreneurial environment is spent on communicating with others. A further break-up of this describes how we invest our time in various aspects of communication:

- 10 per cent of the communication is spent in writing.
- 15 per cent in reading.
- 30 per cent in speaking.
- 45 per cent in listening.

This calculation is based on studies carried out on the routine functioning of executives. In organised seminars, meetings, workshops, etc., the magnitude of time devoted to listening by a larger number of people will expand manifold times. No communication is ever possible in the absence of listening. It is, therefore, extremely important to understand the process of communication and the barriers thereto, because effective communication is vital to give expression to our thoughts (personality) and meaning to our life (existence). In fact, if we ponder a little deeper on the subject, we will realise that effective communication is the highway for all human progress. Without communication, nothing is possible in life! Communication is life. Its absence denotes extinction of life from human body. Imagine a state when you cannot listen nor understand nor speak with people! How terrible you feel when you want to speak but nobody hears!

When you sit in an audience and hear a really good orator glide into peoples' minds, you come out thinking how easy it must be for some people to develop the speech power. To create and enjoy the impact of your communication skills over others makes you yearn for developing some of these qualities of effective communication within yourself. People measure us by what, how and how much we communicate with them, be it through conversation, presentation, speech or formal/informal interaction of any other form.

Shifting workplace and market environments have created a new wave of individual and organisational challenges: rapid promotions, multi-functional partnering and new responsibilities. Not to mention the organisational necessity of conflict resolution, dispute solving, mediation or negotiations on which hinges the whole business of so many organisations and individuals.

Communication skill is the pre-requisite for all other success techniques and, in fact, the very bedrock of our meaningful existence. It is through communication that we connect ourselves to others. None can deny the fact that no individual or group is an island unto himself, i.e. none can exist without communication. Imagine a group of people where one member speaks only Sanskrit and others do not know the language. No transference of ideas and understanding of meaning can be possible in such a situation. Perfect communication — if there were such a thing — entails transfer of a thought or idea in such a way that the mental picture conceived by one is received and perceived by the other, exactly with the same hues and dimensions. When communication is handled carelessly, the intended picture is not established in the receiver's mind. Imagine trying to comprehend a negative or an inverted frame!

EFFECTIVE LISTENING

The most routinely experienced and yet least understood is the significance of listening for building trust and fostering relationships. Listening is not merely an act; it is a valuable social responsibility and etiquette. Even Nature has bestowed *hearing* in us as a faculty of higher precedence over *speaking*. An infant who cannot hear, does not grow up to speak either. Physiologically, the dumb must be deaf too; or he is dumb because he cannot hear. The rest of us started hearing much before we were able to speak. Gradually intellect converted hearing into listening and we started learning, analysing and assimilating wisdom too. A German proverb highlights the virtue of listening very succinctly and softly muffled as: 'Speech is silver but silence is golden; speech is human, silence is divine.'

Transference of wisdom from generation to generation has reached us through oral communication, i.e. careful speaking and listening. All civilisations of the world are built around this tradition of learning. In India, the ancient Vedic civilisation thrived on *shruti* (listening) and *smriti* (recollection/reminiscence). The significance of listening is explained by the fact that *shruti* became synonymous with the Vedas. Even in prayers, listening gets precedence over speaking.

...Shranuyaam sharadah shatam, prabravaam sharadah shatam...

(...Bestow upon me the blessing of good listening for a hundred years; bless me then with the power of effective speaking for a hundred years...).

—Yajur Veda: 3/24

THE ART OF LISTENING

'Know how to listen, and you'll profit even from those who talk badly.'

— Plutarch

You must have seen someone rehearsing his speech or presentation. But have you ever seen anyone practise listening? The answer explains how scant attention we pay to this important aspect. *Speaking* has meaning only if there is *listening*. You cannot be a good speaker unless you become a good listener. Listening is an art that, unfortunately, has been ignored by most of us. Despite the fact that companies spend more time and money developing communication skills than any other management skill, most of us don't communicate well because of our poor listening skills. Good listening involves linking our thoughts with that of the speaker. We will be able to assimilate the speech better, analyse it realistically and, maybe, even arouse fresh curiosity to enquire and know more if we were empathetic to the speaker. It is realised that an average person speaks at a rate of about 150 words per minute, whereas he has the capacity to listen at the rate of over 1,000 words per minute. Obviously, our capacity to assimilate is more than our power to disseminate.

Anyone can develop a pleasing, confident manner of speaking with a well-modulated voice that tells others that he/she is in control and they can feel positive about themselves. Whether the conversation is personal or of social or business nature, the shrewd conversationalist will have a well-developed *listening ability* rather than be only concerned in imposing his/her own views over others. While we may enjoy talking more than we enjoy listening, a prudent person will know how to do both. Listening is not complete unless its following three facets are activated and blended together. These are:

- **Hearing:** It is obviously the first part as nothing in communicative interaction can take off in the absence of hearing. It must be facilitated acoustically, physically and psychologically.
- **Attention:** If we pay attention to *hearing*, we start *listening*. In the absence of attention our faculties perform perfunctorily; for instance, sometimes we are *hearing* but not *listening*; *looking* but not *seeing*; *speaking* but not *communicating*; *munching* but not *eating*; and even more — *thinking* and yet not *feeling*. This perfunctory manner of functioning in life always causes problems — individual and social. Most of the diseases and physical/mental disorders can be traced to this perfunctory style of leading our lives. Likewise, strained relationships will be more specifically found linked to this lack of attention in life.
- **Comprehension**: If we have heard someone with attention, it is certain that we have comprehended the message too.

Our comprehension may give rise to agreement or disagreement with what is being talked, discussed or spoken. We might even be encouraged to voice our opinion, which maybe for or against the subject on hand. But, either way, it is certainly the fruition of our listening to someone.

Swami Dayanand Saraswati, the first torch-bearer who sowed the seeds of Indian freedom movement, and a great social reformer and founder of Arya Samaj, has attached great significance to listening. Listening is one of the means of attaining enlightenment and ultimate emancipation. Proper listening, the Swami explains, is caled *shravana chatushtaya* in Vedic parlance (*Satyartha Prakash,* Chapter 9) and its constituents are:

1. *Shravana* (hearing) is the first step towards effective listening and a prerequisite for proper assimilation. It is the function of the ear.
2. *Manana* (reflecting) means pondering over what one hears in the light of one's own experience and logic. It is the function of the brain. Clarifications must be sought to remove doubts, if any.
3. *Nididhyaasana* (mulling) implies analysing the entire matter received in mind from different angles. Sit down in solitude in *yogic* meditation posture, expand the subject matter and analyse it in the light of your own beliefs, reason and evidence that may be in support or otherwise.
4. *Saakshaatkaara* (manifestation) is the true nature of knowledge that results from mental processes described above and the ultimate understanding and realisation of the subject in its true, real form. This also implies exploring the depths beneath the surface to dispel illusions, if any, and knowing the subject matter in its true form, nature and attributes — as it really is.

It is only after such a realisation that information received converts itself into wisdom in the listener's mind. Until such a realisation is achieved, the information lies in the shelves of the mind without much utility in real life. To avail of it in real life, it must become a component of wisdom that would spring up at the right occasions to help us achieve better results and make life a little better in qualitative reckoning.

Every day around us we hear our elders, children, spouse and colleagues whining alike: 'See, I have been telling; but who listens to me?' Whenever something goes wrong even at national level, opposition party leaders join in a chorus and blame the government for not listening to their advice. *Speaking, telling* and *advising* seem to be in abundance; only *listening* is in short supply. In the absence of listening, there is no flow of communication. It is like a one-way traffic with no feedback, no return. The speaker, therefore, is shooting in the dark. Proper listening goes beyond words. If we are not on the same thinking plane as the speaker, the same words may mean different to different people. It may end up in miscarriage of communication and subsequently to creation of misunderstandings as happened in the case of two senile persons:

A retired professor and his wife were holidaying in a holiday cottage in Goa. The couple was old and supposedly senile too. Joseph D'Souza, the cottage attendant, accompanied them whenever they went out for a walk on the beach. One sunny morning, as they strolled along the shore, a seagull flew low and dropped a blob of excrement, which landed right on top of the bald head of the professor. D'Souza saw what happened and said with concern: "Wait right here. I'll get some toilet paper."

As the attendant ran towards the cottage, the professor's wife turned to her husband and pointing towards D'Souza said, "He's a fool. That seagull will be a mile away by the time D'Souza gets back with the toilet paper!"

EFFECT OF INFORMATION EXPLOSION ON LISTENING

Advancement in the technological field has placed the world on an unprecedented fast track. We find ourselves in the midst of a highly mobile multitude. Call it a mad race, a rat race or what you will, we have to keep pace not only to protect ourselves from being crushed in the stampede, but also to achieve higher goals. There is an abundance of information and technological resources around. We are globally connected and everything is happening right in front of our eyes. Communication technology has shrunk the world to such an extent that the farthest corner of the world lies right across our window. Fleeting opportunities are being slurped through fierce competition. Multi-channel TVs, satellite communication, cell-phones, Internet, FM radio — all keep on feeding us with unlimited information, non-stop. How much can one be attentive, and to what? Reading a newspaper while having breakfast and watching TV at the same time — it is not uncommon to find such a scene. There are some of us who carry newspapers and phones to the toilet too. Wanting to accumulate too much in too short a time! This has led us to a state of *split attention*. Unconsciously we keep on discarding so much out of the humdrum of activities buffeting us from all directions.

It is impossible to listen to all sources of information and knowledge. Also, we need to protect ourselves from such intense information explosion. Psychologically we all develop our peculiar protective mechanisms against it. We have, therefore, unconsciously adapted ourselves to modern life's pragmatism. We have chosen our distinctive lanes on this superhighway of modern communication and opportunities.

We have adopted individualised methods to listen selectively to things of our interest while turning a deaf ear — psychological earmuffs — to what we consider trivial or irrelevant. And this has been happening to us unconsciously.

COMMON IMPEDIMENTS TO GOOD LISTENING

- **Environmental factors:** The ambience has an important significance. Lack of proper arrangements can divert our attention. Physical discomfort too may distract us from the talk for which we primarily gather. Imagine yourself as part of the audience in the following environment:
  - Poor lighting, acoustics and uncomfortable seating arrangements.
  - Distracting noise of outside traffic, repair work in the adjacent room/building or commotion of some kind.
  - Too warm or cold weather with scant thought paid to heating or cooling arrangements.
  - Glare of sun; dusty, gusty winds; poorly done up visuals and other paraphernalia.
  - Unnecessary movement of liaison, service staff.
  - Too flashy or too unkempt accoutrements of liaison, service staff.
  - Atmosphere filled with the aroma of refreshments being served or laid out in near vicinity.
- **Absence of motivational factors:** We can hear something without wanting to hear; but we cannot listen to anything

without wanting to listen. We must have a keen desire to learn more and the faith to gain from listening to the speaker. When this faith dwindles, the listening withers. The following points deserve attention:

- Inadequate publicity to the speaker and subject may not invoke enough enthusiasm in the audience to learn something new.
- Speaker's background may be unimpressive to kindle curiosity.
- Our own expertise in the subject being higher than that of the speaker — or if so we believe — we are unlikely to be drawn to listen to him/her.
- Unfamiliarity with the subject of speech/discussion may keep us switched off.
- A preconceived notion that such talks are mere periodical rituals without any worthwhile gain will plug our listening faculty with psychological earmuffs.

- **Poor anchoring:** Every individual has his attention span. No one is attentive for unlimited time, whatever the subject and whosoever the speaker. It is, therefore, for the speaker to take care and keep the audience anchored to his/her theme by rejuvenating their interest from time to time. Short, crisp and well-prepared presentation/speech laced with humour will keep the audience well anchored to you. Some of the reasons why listening drifts occur:
  - Platitudes, harangues and abstract explanations tend to bore the audience.
  - Too long lectures wean away the listeners from the main theme.
  - Lack of audio-visual aids and monotony in the method of talk makes the atmosphere dull.

  - Failure of the speaker to show the benefits that listeners will get from the talk will keep the listening enthusiasm low.
  - Lack of interactive or participative approach often results in failure to connect the speaker to the audience.
- **Individual predilections and prejudices:** Psychologically we have a protective mechanism that protects us from unpleasant or painful ingresses. This mechanism sifts the matter and lets in only the favourable inputs; all that is unfavourable is kept out. How strong or flexible this mechanism is will depend on the quality of our predilections and prejudices, which may further be compounded by emotions, apprehensions, fears, suspicions and desires. It is due to this reason that opposition party MPs find it difficult to listen to a minister's explanation and vice-versa in TV interviews. It is also because of personal prejudices that the leader of a labour union does not listen to a manager; a rich man does not listen to a poor man's advice; teenagers do not want to listen to elders' talk. Everyone wants to hold on to his/her own cherished ideas. The fear of abandoning these cherished ideas activates the protective mechanism.
- **Rebuttal instinct:** In conversations and discussions one's prestige sometimes becomes an issue. When this happens, we stop listening and, instead, get busy planning to refute and rebut everything that the speaker is saying. Our aim becomes *'demolish his theory'*, no matter how realistic or logical it is. We do come across people who are always against new ideas or change and will be ever ready to rebut any new idea even before evaluating it. They favour the status quo for it is the easiest thing to stay and stagnate, rather than take the risk to change. Even during the

freedom struggle of India, there were many Rai Bahadurs who did not want the change and did everything possible to demolish the idea of *swaraj*. Their strongest and perennial arguments were: 'Has it ever happened?'; 'We never had it this way here,'; 'He's just been here six months and has started challenging the age-old practices we have been following all these years...' Such arguments destroy meetings and presentations. The speaker has to evolve a strategy on how to sell his/her ideas to such unwilling listeners. Arguments and counter-arguments do not help. Subsequent sessions to discuss case studies, brain-storming sessions and intelligently devised games will be more useful to get the unwilling people into a proper frame of mind.

HOW TO IMPROVE LISTENING POWER?

Psychologists say that an average human brain is capable of assimilating 1,000 words per minute whereas he/she is capable of speaking 150 words per minute. This phenomenon leaves a gap between what has been said and what has been ingested. The brain craves for more to fill up the vacuum of a capacity of about 850 more words. It cannot remain inactive. It, therefore, starts analysing the matter already received. In doing so, it may start comparing the information with that already in store. Sometimes, the brain may pick up an idea that can spin off other ideas, shooting completely out of orbit the talk at hand. In dealing with the information, the human brain may behave in one of the three typical ways:

- **Empty mind:** For such a mind, sifting is not an important activity. It stores anything and everything that can be stuffed into it. Such a mind lacks analytical ability and, though it may contain immense information, it would not be able to utilise it for optimal gains. It is like a junkyard where useful instruments and scrap lie, rusting together. It is more prone to gullibility and lacks power of discretion and analysis.

- **Closed mind:** It is totally opposite of the first type. Nothing is allowed to enter, except for one's own narrow ideas. It is a frog-of-the-well scenario in which the self-centred attitudes bundle up themselves and resist everything alien. No worthwhile listening is possible in this case as the negative forces push out everything external.
- **Open mind:** It is the awakened type and is alive to the happenings around. It has the ability to sift, analyse and classify the information received. Its discerning power makes it function more actively, empowering itself further with good listening. It does not allow individual predilections and prejudices to colour perceptions or come in the way of expanding one's horizons.

Obviously, it is the open mind that gains the maximum from listening. To keep the mind open and focused on the talk, conscious effort is required. Here are some tips that will help you gain a lot from listening consciously and consequently building up knowledge, tolerance and even interpersonal relationships:

- **Don't interrupt:** You can either talk or listen. Give your ear to the speaker. Let him/her deliver his/her message completely without interruption. Even if you think otherwise and feel that he/she is unlikely to enlist your support or approval, exercise restraint until you have heard him/her fully.
- **Encourage the talker:** Help him/her to talk freely to you. An encouraging and permissive environment is necessary to help the talker express his/her ideas or opinion. This way

you are more likely to receive a better response and understand his/her meaning better and quickly.

- **Evince interest:** Make conscious effort to look and act interested in the person talking to you and in his/her talk. Reading newspapers or mail, watching TV, surfing Internet, talking on phone, supervising or passing instructions to others while he/she is discussing, making submissions or recommendations to you debars you from effective listening. Besides being bad etiquette, such activities put off the speaker.
- **Create favourable ambience:** If the place of your meeting is abuzz with multifarious activities, like shifting of stores, repair work going on, too much of staff activity, etc., the talker as well as the listener are bound to be distracted. Remove the distractions and create a conducive atmosphere to motivate interaction during the talk, discussion or presentation.
- **Invoke the great virtue of empathy:** Let your face, body and gestures convey to the talker that you are able to see what he/she wants to show. Even if the other person's point of view is not in sync with yours, you will be in a better position to evaluate it objectively if you hear it empathetically. Someone has aptly said that 'listening requires two ears, one for meaning and one for feeling'.
- **Practise patience:** Try to give enough time and let the talker exhaust himself/herself. A feeling that you have listened to someone fully will itself be enough motivation for striking effective communication. Signs of boredom and impatience will damage this effectiveness.
- **Control your anger and whims:** Whims tend to resist reason. Anger encourages conceit and addiction to

preconceived ideas. In such a scenario wrong meanings are deduced from right expressions. Tolerance and magnanimity are qualities we must practise at all times.

- **Exhibit curiosity:** Genuine curiosity will keep the mind focused on the talk. Ask relevant questions; this will encourage the other person to progress with the point further. It also convinces him/her that you are listening.
- **Discuss; don't condemn:** While a discussion encourages communication, condemnation and rejection desist the talker, who becomes defensive. Difference of opinion should be expressed to know more on the subject rather than to belittle and make the other person clam up.
- **Stop talking:** Talking is *pushing* out words. Listening is akin to *pulling*. You cannot *pull* and *push* at the same time; for if you do that, you achieve nothing. It is, therefore, necessary to stop talking for better listening. Silence, too, is an art in itself. It is invaluable because it affords you time and space to reflect on what someone is saying and what he or she means.

Besides facilitating learning and understanding, listening is a courtesy we show others even when the topic of conversation is not of our choice. A good listener listens for hidden meanings behind the words, but is careful not to read the wrong meaning into what is being said. Decision makers, who do not listen, have less information for making sound decisions. Therefore, not only what we say is important, but also how we say and how we listen are equally important for effective communication.

Abraham Lincoln, an icon of success, who rose from humble beginnings to become President of USA, once said, "When I am getting ready to reason with a man, I spend one-third of my time thinking about myself and what I am going to say — and two-thirds thinking about him and what he is going to say."

Making Others Listen to You

'The art of conversation consists as much in listening politely as in speaking agreeably.'

— Atwell

Add on to Your Knowledge

It is essential to sift and organise the substance of the speech or the presentation. But that is possible only when we have sufficient knowledge of the subject. It is, therefore, very useful to develop and maintain a regular reading habit. If reading is followed by discussion with one endowed with the ability to question or contribute something useful, the information so gathered will be easily converted to knowledge. Likewise, if we were to write a commentary on our readings, we would find that we have not only gained from the author whose work we read, but also our own ideas have multiplied, blended and enriched our knowledge. Even in our routine conversations, we will find that if our viewpoint is supplemented by knowledge thus gained, people will be more inclined to talk and listen to us.

Prepare Your Talk Well

There is a fallacy among most people that only formal speech or presentations need prior preparation and rehearsal. On the contrary, thoughtful preparation is a prerequisite of all communication, be it formal or informal. Often, we realise its importance only after the damage has been done. The cases given below highlight the importance of prior preparation in all kinds of talks. In fact, these are the communication problems that most of us face in our daily life:

1. Smita was the only daughter of her parents. A brilliant girl, she was the apple of her father's eyes. In her final year at college, she fell in love with Raman, her class-fellow, who hailed from Chennai. Smita decided to tell her parents all about it. When she blurted out her affair to her mother, the latter was shell-shocked. As she suffered from hypertension, she had to be hospitalised. Smita's father felt bad too. There was no approval to this relationship.
2. Christopher Ekka was a senior executive in a brewery. Known for his efficiency, he commanded a lot of respect. At the conclusion of a meeting chaired by the General Manager wherein new policies were explained, he was asked to offer his views about the changes proposed. Christopher expressed his reservations and questioned the very wisdom of the proposed changes. His criticism not only hurt the feelings of the Manager who felt hurt, but even the Study Team, that had studied and worked out the proposed changes after prolonged in-depth research, turned hostile to him.
3. A team of doctors and nurses from Delhi visited a remote Rajasthan village to impart health education and promote population control among the villagers. The Rural Family Welfare Camp, as the venture was called, took off amidst much fanfare. The senior physician got up to give a talk to the villagers. He started finding fault with everything: "You know nothing about sex. You villagers have no idea about how a woman conceives. I will now explain to you with the help of this chart how the ovum forms, travels through the fallopian tube to the uterus and waits there to fertilise after meeting the sperm..." He was not allowed to proceed any

further. The entire medical team was hounded out of the village.

4. Naik Abdul Raza, who had no real problem at home, managed to get leave even when there was a ban on leave in the Army due to troop deployment on the border with Pakistan. Havildar Yudhvir Singh, a Jat from Haryana, had his wife lying in a critical state, battling for life in a hospital in Chandigarh. He failed to convince his company Commander about his sorry plight and was denied leave.
5. Pratap Singh Daulta, a political leader of unified Punjab, was vehemently opposed to Pratap Singh Kairon who headed the Congress government in Punjab in the 1950s. Pratap Singh Daulta took the Jat electorate by storm and even succeeded in mobilising strong public opinion against the Congress by levelling baseless charges, which the illiterate masses blindly believed. Kairon and Congress were gobbling up all the credit for Nangal Hydel Project and Bhakra Dam that provided farmers water through the newly constructed canals. "What Bhakra Dam? What canals? Do you fellows know what flows through these canals?" Daulta asked the farmers' rally. "What remains after you churn the milk and take the butter out of it? All the power — electricity — that could add vigour to your crops has been taken out of the water at Bhakra Dam. What you are getting in the shape of water is lifeless liquid that would render your fields infertile, into torrid tracts of wasteland after a few years!" And, lo behold, the gullible farmers became so angry at this that they voted against the Congress. Of course, Daulta could not ride high for long on such tales.

In Case No. 1, Smita could not make her parents listen to her.

She had not given a thought to the desires and dreams of her parents. She had merely thought of herself and refused to listen to them. Had Smita known the stand her parents were likely to take, she could have soft-pedalled the talk and gradually influenced them and invoked their blessings through tactful and convincing talk.

In Case No. 2, Christopher Ekka had every right to differ from the rest. Only the tactless and crude criticism of the new proposal was too brash. As a responsible senior executive of the company, he should have exercised restraint in condemning outright the new policy that was an offshoot of the recommendations made by the Study Team. He not only failed in making the General Manager and others listen to his observations, but also spoiled his relations with his seniors and other colleagues.

In Case No. 3, the doctor spoke from the book without taking into account the sentiments and culture of the villagers. He failed to motivate them to listen to him. In fact, his observations about their lifestyle seemed to humiliate them, which they could not tolerate; hence, the revolt.

In Case No. 4, Naik Abdul Raza succeeded in putting across his story in a persuasive manner that convinced his company Commander about the compassion his story invoked. Yudhvir Singh, on the other hand, was not used to displaying his personal worries and anxiety, especially that concerning his wife, in public. He, therefore, put across his story very plainly. Bare facts and no emotion failed to elicit a sympathetic response.

In Case No 5, Pratap Singh Daulta had planned his talk to mislead the gullible farmers by astutely twisting the truth. He chose the language carefully, coloured the facts very shrewdly and used their emotions imaginatively against an assumed enemy for a short-term gain. He succeeded, though dishonestly, in making people listen and believe even the most illogical story he sold out.

DEVELOP INTEREST IN PEOPLE

It is good manners as well as an effective strategy to take genuine interest in people. This will enable you to establish an easy rapport with them; you will be able to connect better to them and understand their views properly. The subject under discussion may or may not be of your interest. If it is of your interest, you will naturally be drawn into the conversation. If the subject is not, your interest in the person and the overall situation at hand will enable you to endure the goings on. A little curiosity on your part to acquaint yourself with the new subject or the other's viewpoint will help you learn something new and protect you from getting isolated from the group.

There is a wise saying, 'Great talent for conversation should be accompanied with great politeness. He who eclipses others owes them great civilities; and, whatever mistaken vanity may tell us, it is better to please in conversation than to shine in it.'

Interest in others will help build relations and expand your area of influence over a larger section of the society. Greater tolerance on your part will surprise you by opening up new vistas of knowledge because when you follow the social grace of sharing ideas and thoughts with others, you will soon learn something new about subjects and problems that were hitherto unknown to you. Consequently, you will be able to contribute constructively in meetings, discussions and negotiations more as also effectively than ever before.

RESPECT EMOTIONS AND ADD FEELINGS

In organisational environments as well as in a social milieu, transaction of feelings and information acts like the glue that binds people together. The process through which such a bond is established is called *communication*. Bad communication or absence of good communication can lead to a breakdown in systems and relationships, subsequently resulting in losses, damages and legal/social problems. Therefore, communication is not only the flow of information; it is also the flow of attitudes, ideas and opinions. It involves the transmission of feelings and desires; it is a systematic process of telling, listening and understanding. Everyone wants to be heard, recognised and respected as an individual. It is through communication that we convey to our listeners in what esteem we hold them. Diplomatic and tactful talking may connect and help develop relations. Brash and brazen talking, likewise, may cause short circuit and sparks that may damage relations.

'Nothing is more silly than the pleasure some people take in 'speaking their minds'. A man of this make will say a rude thing, for the mere pleasure of saying it, when an opposite behaviour, full of innocence, might have preserved his friend, or made his fortune.'

— Steele

SPEAK WITH CONVICTION

Oral communication is successful when it boosts interest and spurs a genuine resonance between the persons communicating with each other. It should be complete both in letter and spirit — each letter being the product of spirit and gliding straight into the innate being of the listener. When we speak what we truly believe, our ideas acquire real existence, definite shape and dimension for the listener. When so laced with conviction, the information we convey becomes easily assimilable, accessible and acceptable.

Whenever the custodian of ideas hesitates, his/her self-doubt becomes evident and others suspect him/her. So, the ideas do not sell because the quality is doubted. On the other hand, when the information is presented with conviction, the message becomes clear, unambiguous and convincing. However, lack of precision, distortion of meaning, superimposition of one's prejudices and complexes in the message may create problems in communicating with each other. Such a communication is not only incomplete, it becomes counterproductive too. For achieving effective listening, faith in one's own ideas, thoughts and beliefs is most essential.

Intonation and Voice Inflection

The human voice is a unique instrument. Unless physically impaired, each one of us can achieve wonderful results with the voice. Voice control allows us to deliver our message to produce the effect we wish to achieve. Intonation means change or variation in the tone, including inflection and accent to cast an impact on the audience. A simple word like 'no' can convey different meanings with varying impact. An emphatic and sharp 'no' means disagreement or refusal. A curt 'no' may just mean disinterest or decline. A curious 'no' will seek support or agreement to what we say rather than meaning anything else. The word is same, but the intonation gives it many colours. Intonation is very important to convey the right meaning with desired impact. The tone, pitch and volume blended with requisite sharpness, softness, solemnity, and even rhetoric, have their own relevance and significance depending on what we are talking about, whom we are addressing and on what occasion we are talking. This helps in making the delivery smooth, interesting and meaningful.

Correct breathing and posture help to extend the range of voice inflections. It also helps prevent strain and imparts the voice with the necessary vitality required. In addition, good articulation helps us make the speech clear and distinct. Voice inflection enables us to highlight important words and phrases and makes it easier for the listener to comprehend the meaning. To avoid monotony in a voice, inflection is necessary. Further, the use of pace and pause imparts character to speech.

Remember, voice is a wonder tool at our disposal. We can fine-tune it and its flow can submerge listeners in its melody. On the other hand, its bare crudeness can put off listeners so badly that we may end up in serious embarrassment. If accompanied by crude phonetics and language too, the combination can be disastrous.

Henry Giles has this to say about the significance of voice inflection: 'Never is the deep, strong voice of man, or the low sweet voice of woman, finer than in the earnest but mellow tones of familiar speech, richer than the richest music, which are a delight, while they are heard, which linger still upon the ear in softened echoes, and which, when they have ceased, come, long after, back to memory, like the murmurs of a distant hymn.'

ENGLISH PRONUNCIATION: PHONETICS AND ACCENTS

Unlike other languages, proficiency in written English does not guarantee proficiency in spoken English. This is because of the phonetic complexity of English language. There is little correlation between letters and sound. Sometimes letters do not have distinct sounds; a letter or even a group of them may remain silent or a single letter may have different sounds. The way a person pronounces depends on his/her mother tongue, environment and exposure.

English pronunciation of Indians is largely accepted as good. But this is so only in case of those who have had the benefit of good public or convent schooling. There are many among us who require training and improvement, no matter how good we are in grammar and how rich is our vocabulary. Some of the defects we have are: regional twang, improper accents, influence of local dialect and mother tongue that either hastens or drags, creating a mismatch between the voice and the words.

A more serious drawback that is noticed in some people is unreasonable obsession to find the most proper, perhaps even a high-sounding, word for a simple expression. It is something like what happens with some Hindi bigots who dig out Sanskrit and Hindi dictionaries to find the most appropriate translation of English words that are in common use, for words like school, train, station, pen, park and so on. It really looks absurd. At least in India, the present society is already acknowledging the most pragmatic communication style — Hinglish—which is becoming popular in speeches and presentations too.

Minor flaws notwithstanding, I insist that you need not be overly concerned about the high points of grammar and vocabulary. Too much stress on these matters may invite ridicule, rather than adulation.

This is precisely what happened to K.P. Singh, a neo-rich businessman from Bihar who had developed an impressively rich English vocabulary. He had long craved to visit London and the countryside of England since the days of his childhood when he had read 'Mr Pickwick' as a student in a Government High School, Maner, near Danapur.

'Someday, maybe,' he had fantasised, 'I too would travel in horse-drawn carriages on roads of London, tread the same paths and stop on those very country inns where Pickwickian characters moved around.'

The day finally arrived when he was invited to London by one of his friends who admired him for his progress and was a senior official at the Indian High Commission in London. The friend understood and respected K.P. Singh's love for English and England.

A day after his arrival in London, K.P. Singh was introduced to a number of English friends, including some dignitaries, at a dinner party. His sincere and simple disposition impressed quite a few. He made new friends whom he met off and on in the market, library or restaurant. One of them joined K.P. Singh in his morning walks. "You look sad, Mr K.P.," said Martin, the newfound English friend, one morning. "Any problems?"
"Well, Mr Martin, I am having trouble with my wife."

"Oh, no!" said Martin, "That's sad. But I thought you loved your wife very much."
"Oh yes," said K.P. Singh, "I love her very, very much."
"Then what is the trouble?"
"Well," K.P. said, "we very much want to have some children, and... er ...my wife seems to be... how do you say? Umm ...yeah! ...unbearable!"
"Unbearable?" asked Martin.
"No, not that way..." K.P. tried to clarify, "I mean, ummm... er... what do you call it? Yeah...inconceivable."
Still a blank expression on Martin's face.
"Oh ho, what I mean, you see," K.P. attempted again but compounded Martin's confusion further, "is that she is... uh... umm... oh yes, that's it... impregnable!"

Even if K.P. Singh could not get the right word — infertility or barrenness — there are ways on how to convey the idea in a simpler, clearer way. Obsession with language, or pedantic adherence to petty details kills communication and mostly backfires, giving way to ridicule and mockery.

NON-VERBAL COMMUNICATION AND KINESICS

The study of communication through body language is called *kinesics*. At times, we conduct the most persuasive and crucial communication non-verbally, through a gesture, accent, intonation, posture or even facial expression. Body language is our 'give away'. Most of us are not aware of our gestures, postures and quirks that are all apparent to the person with whom we are interacting. We all have experience of occasions when we did not take someone's words seriously because his/her facial expression betrayed his/her oral statement. There is generally a dissonance between words and body movements when we say something we do not really believe. And, there is perfect harmony between body and speech when we speak what we really mean.

Body movements do convey feelings and inclinations of individuals to some extent. But while body movements accompanied by verbal communication do heighten the expression, unconscious movements inadvertently convey that which may be misread. Hence, interpretations may not always be conclusive for all individuals across the board.

It is, therefore, important to be completely engrossed in a communication — voice, eyes, face, hands and arms, with all of your physical self — assisting in what you have to say. Eye contact with the audience and effective use of gestures are the most powerful tools of non-verbal accompaniments to human communication.

How does our body help in improving our communication skills and the effect of our message? Communication takes place through varied modes:

- **Facial expressions:** Face mirrors the emotions of an individual. Obliquely tilted face, withdrawn chin, fixed gaze and hard pressed lips convey our disapproval of what is being talked. On the other hand, chin jutting out, face craning out, lips relaxed or nearly open with head somewhat bowing and pulling the upper body forward would be indicative of a keen interest in the person and the topic at hand.
- **Eyes:** Eyes convey a whole lot of information; at times more

than even what words convey. A single glance can convey a message that would require tons of language. A wink, twinkle, gleam or a sparkle in the eyes instantly conveys the interest and approval, whereas a stare, gaze, ogle, or a peering eye shows how intently one is examining the issue. A sneer, a scorn or dislike is so vividly expressed by eyes that even efforts to hide it betray the truth. Sly, furtive, leering look invites such wrath that a serious problem can crop up, despite not a word being uttered.

- **Hand movements:** Clasped hands indicate a defensive posture. Hands hanging or swinging, as if involuntarily, betray nervousness. Tapping fingers on the table, squeezing palms or twitching fingers is an expression of worry and anxiety. Hands rising to emphasise a point in the speech express confidence.
- **Leg movements:** If you are sitting and shaking your legs or tapping toes on the floor, it indicates you are not very interested in whatever is going on. If standing with legs too close, perhaps, you are nervous. If you are on one leg with the other leg kept loose, you are trying to overcome your fear. Uneven pace with laboured movements also betrays lack of confidence. A confident posture would be to sit normally with both legs together, with feet resting on the floor, straight under the front edge of the chair. When standing, stand on both your legs with feet kept normally apart. If you are required to pace up and down in front of an audience, do it with your body upright, brisk pace and deliberate.
- **Body posture:** A crouched torso, drooping shoulders and gawky deportment convey your lack of confidence. Keep your torso straight, shoulders pulled back, chest up and

chin parallel to the ground. Even when you sit, practise sitting upright; avoid slumping and reclining in your chair or sofa.

- **Spatial distance and orientation:** If you get too close to people, you seem invasive and obscene. If on the other hand, you remain too far away, you give the impression of disinterest in the people and issue being discussed. An arm's length is a good distance that honourable people maintain. Allow elbowroom to your neighbours when sitting on a dining table or in a crowd.

Gesturing can relax you, reinforce your message and make your speech more striking and your presentation more interesting to watch. In addition, there are some fringe areas such as clothes, physique, general appearance, etc. that add to the overall effect.

'Such as thy words are, so will thine affections be esteemed; and such as thine affections, will be thy deeds; and such as thy deeds will be thy life.'

— Socrates

Focus 2: Making Others Listen to You!

- It is through good listening that you get a peep into the other person's personality. It wins concern and goodwill too! Listen fully, even if you disagree totally.
- Genuine interest in people, organisation and the situation will enhance the effect of your speaking.
- Avoid gossip. Talk ideas and concepts.
- Make sure your listener is relaxed and free to listen to you.
- Think first on what you want to say. Formulate and polish the idea in your mind to see it absolutely clearly.

(Contd.)

- Then break the idea in parts, if need be; and deliver it clearly, briefly, and confidently.
- If you are to describe an event or put across a proposal, give the boss a general framework to enable him/her to be prepared for what to anticipate from you.
- In describing happenings, proceed in a chronological order. For proposals, a logical order leading to recommendations would be more appropriate.
- Encourage questions to make the communication a two-way transaction.
- Your body language, voice and etiquette will be largely responsible for creating an effect on the audience.

SPECIFIC ACTION PLAN

A - How many times in the last quarter have you spoken out of turn to interrupt someone's talk during meetings or informal/social gatherings?

____

____

____

____

____

____

B - What was the reaction of people on this and what did you achieve?

____

____

____

____

____

____

C - Write down the names of the people whom you like to listen to with joy and rapt attention.

D - What are the reasons for your enjoying their conversation or oratory?

E - Select topics of your choice. Rehearse and record speaking in front of a mirror today (a three-minute speech to an imaginary audience). Then rewind and play the cassette to yourself. Yes, some of it you may admire and some you won't. List out the improvements you want to achieve in your public speaking.

F - This month select three occasions where you will interact with different people and actively participate in meetings — social service groups, community meetings, club functions, etc. From next month onwards participate in at least one such interaction once a month.

G - Volunteer your services for people-related extra responsibilities in your office.

> Conversation should be pleasant without scurrility, witty without affectation, free without indecency, learned without conceitedness, novel without falsehood.
>
> — Shakespeare

3

Business Meetings, Presentations and Public Speaking

How easy do you find it to strike a conversation with a complete stranger? It is not easy when you have no idea what the other person likes or how he/she feels about things because you are unaware of his/her background, profession, education, political leanings, individual preferences and the like. Contrast it with a group of friends who love to talk. How easy do you find it to join in, to make interesting conversation with people you know? Perhaps, you even have arrangement to meet only for conversation very regularly. Coffee-house meetings and discussions have often blossomed into deep relationships. But, even for these friendly groups, there was a starting time from which they grew into influential groups, mooting great ideas.

The ability to listen has relevance here too. It is easy to nod and pretend that you are fascinated by what they are saying, but if you do no more than that, you would hardly bear the conversation for long. Perhaps, besides getting bored yourself, you would put off others too. It is your indulgence in the conversation that will integrate you into the group and the topic of conversation. You need to ask questions. Your indulgence will help you to ask pertinent questions. Most people love to talk about themselves and their interests; so if you can ask questions on their favourite topic, you are likely to hold their interest.

Patrick Henry was more impressed by Washington's quiet conversation than by the clever oratory of others. When asked whom he considered the greatest man in the Congress, he replied: "Rutledge, if you speak of eloquence, is by far the greatest orator, but Colonel Washington, who has no pretensions to eloquence, is a man of more solid judgement and information than any man on that floor." Tools of affectation are thus redundant if you are empowered by knowledge, sincerity and conviction. Ego is an important part of an individual's personality. If you can't please it, you have no right to hurt it. The risk in talking too much is threefold: one, the main point loses thrust in the deluge of chatter; two, you expose yourself too much; three, you increase your chances of annoying the other party. Colton advises, "When in the company of sensible men, we ought to be doubly cautious of talking too much, lest we lose two good things — their good opinion and our own improvement; for what we have to say we know, but what they have to say we know not." To get it out of them, you will have to ask questions and encourage them to talk.

You might wonder as to what questions could be asked, and if, instead of listening to them, your mind is occupied with your own concerns, your questions may not be pertinent to what they are saying. If your questions appear like an interrogation, the conversation won't flow smoothly. Listen carefully; their words will give you a clue to what to ask. If you are genuinely interested in the goings on, you won't need to bother about what to say, ask and how. So, the pre-requisite is: Develop interest in what is going on. A little patience and listening will provide you some new ideas and your interest will grow, giving rise to curiosity.

For example, if there is a keen golfer talking about his/her sport and you hate golf but love landscape gardening, you can initiate the discussion by asking, "Where do you play?" And when he/she answers, you can lead the conversation with a follow-up question, such as "I've never been there; what is the landscaping of the course like?"

You may find yourself amidst a group of businesspersons you have met sometime ago, but can't remember much about them. You can ask "How's the business running?" When they reply, you can empathise with appropriate phrases, such as "Sounds like you're very busy." All these responses encourage people to talk and feel that you're interested in what they have to say.

For driving the conversation further, you need to get past the facts and turn to opinions and feelings. You can start with "What is/are . . .? Where do you . . .? When did you . . .? Who else is . . .? How many . . .?" If you want someone's opinion or feelings, your questions may be like: "How do you feel . . ." or "What do you find most . . ." or "What do you say about . . .?"

For example, you could ask, the golfer, "Which is your favourite course?" or "Which is the best course on which you have ever played?"

Listen to the golfer's words and ask follow-up questions based on what he or she could have said. You can attune your questions by summarising several points made earlier: "You were saying you travel a lot; what's the most interesting place you've visited?"

By listening carefully and asking relevant questions, you will be amazed at what all you can learn. And, of course, when you are in conversation with other people, you'll have your facts readily available to share!

You can plan, design and deliver a speech to an audience in a packed hall. It is entirely up to you to decide what could be the subject of your speech because speech delivery is largely unidirectional. But, during a conversation where communication is multi-directional, as happens in casual and social gatherings, most conversations drift along. You join in bit by bit, until a point comes where one of the participants takes the reigns and leads the communication in his/her cherished direction.

Effective Communication in Management

How good and effective are you in convincing people? Are rivalries and jealousies straining relations between key individuals or departments, and consequently slowing down productivity? Do personal ambitions overshadow organisational goals because of one-upmanship games? Do problems simmer, even though the situation is under control? Are there rumours of harassment or discrimination? Are new responsibilities overburdening the more competent Managers?

If you answered 'yes' to any of these questions, it would be an indicator of failing communication and widening of communication gap which is bound to give rise to speculation, rumours, mistrust and disloyalty that can be disastrous for organisations — from corporates to small business. Families and social relations can be ruined if such an atmosphere seeps in and persists. For healthy relations and efficiency in all human endeavours, communication is the real key to success. Besides informal conversations, the spectrum of communication can be so complex that we have to categorise and compartmentalise it in various categories:

- *Direct communication:* meetings, presentations, speeches, interviews, negotiations, informal conversations, etc.
- *Indirect communication:* project reports, specially assigned papers, study reports, letters, applications, circulars, notices, etc.

In an organisation, communication patterns assume most of these forms. However, any form of communication is necessarily a social intercourse among people, especially in direct communication where the fallouts are direct and immediate too. Hence, the behavioural aspect cannot be neglected. This is best understood by the three-ego states explained by Eric Berne, i.e. the *parent*, the *child* and the *adult*, wherein the *felt, taught* and *thought* behavioural patterns are exhibited, resulting in parallel, complementary, or crossed communication patterns. The same can be judged by unique voice tones, types of words used, postures, facial expressions and body gestures.

Refining and periodical review through organised training is not merely advisable, but extremely necessary for capable executives, managers and professionals who don't have experienced mentors, up-through-the-ranks training, or fine-tuned people-skills always at hand.

Business Meetings

Any organisation where people are involved, meetings become an integral function. Meetings are not only an information-regulatory mechanism; they act as instruments for discovering and sharing new ideas and finalise policies, mobilise resources, co-ordinate effort, inform and guide people to achieve common goals. Ironically, however, meetings are disliked and mocked at by some, because they usually prove futile, boring, time wasting, dull and inconvenient. If you were to discreetly observe the proceedings, you would find that some of the participants do nothing but doodle with their pen or pencil while a hyper-energetic manager is busy extolling the virtues of his/her previously misunderstood idea.

Your challenge now is to demolish this mould and make your meeting effective and fruitful. As with every other well-conceived and planned management activity, meetings must be planned beforehand, monitored for effectiveness, and reviewed afterwards for evolving and strengthening a better communication platform.

Some of the ideas below may seem too precise in an easy-going, relaxed, semi-informal team atmosphere. However, if you are keen to gain a reputation for holding decisive and effective meetings, then not only will the people value this efficiency but the meetings will prove a fruitful mechanism for enhancing the productivity and performance, besides ensuring smooth co-ordination at all levels.

Meetings take away the participants from their main work with their absence making the work lie in abeyance. It is, therefore, prudent to find answers to the three basic questions before you plan your next meeting:

- What is the agenda of the meeting?
- Who should attend the meeting?
- What should be the frequency and duration of the meeting?

Formulating the Agenda

The purpose of an agenda is to inform the participants of the subject of the meeting, so that they prepare for it well in advance. This helps in structuring and streamlining the discussion and maintaining it within the requisite parameters. It is good to circulate a draft agenda and ask for suggestion of any other business well before the intended meeting. It will ensure that all concerned are informed beforehand. In fact, people must be encouraged to sponsor their ideas and additional agenda points, if any. Such encouragement gives people a sense of importance and belonging. Even if all the sponsored points are not included in the final agenda, such contribution will give you an insight into the minds of the participants. You will know better what could be brewing, where it could be leading and why!

Subsequently, the agenda of the meeting should be finalised and circulated yet again: this time with specific guidelines, responsibilities (for presentations, if any) and time-frame. If you know in advance that a particular participant either needs information or will be providing information, then make this explicitly clear so that there is no confusion.

The business of the meeting, stated in the agenda, should be precise and concise. This form of publicity will emphasise to all that the meeting is about achieving defined goals.

List of Participants

This question requires you to consider the import and applicability of the content of the meeting. Too many cooks spoil the broth. A meeting too, attended by all and sundry, runs the risk of getting derailed from its track. In India, there are many of us who speak too volubly to suggest policies and projects, particularly when we know it is not our responsibility and that the implementation of programmes is someone else's responsibility. The circular carrying the agenda should nominate the authorities or representatives who are required to attend. Instructions can be given as to who will be required to prepare what, so that the participants turn up fully prepared and equipped to make useful contributions at the meeting.

Anyone who is not involved in either planning, co-ordinating or implementing the matter to be discussed, has no business to be present at the meeting, else he/she would be an obstruction to the proceedings; his goodwill, loyalty and fairness notwithstanding.

It is not a waste of time to organise a mass meeting once in a year or so, involving all people from top to bottom. Such meetings or gatherings can constitute a part of the annual functions. The purpose of such mass meetings should be to inform everyone about the overall health, progress and future plans in outline for their organisation. Schemes instituted or planned for the welfare of the employees by the management should also be highlighted in such meetings.

FREQUENCY AND DURATION OF MEETINGS

Too frequent meetings have been found wasteful in respect of time and effort. At the same time, organisations where people do not share the vision of the management, suffer from lack of loyalty and involvement. Whereas routine meetings to review, monitor and guide general functioning of the organisation should have a pre-planned schedule spread out through the year, say, once a quarter or so, additional meetings may be warranted for the following reasons:

- Short notice meetings to find immediate solution to an emergency.
- To discuss effects of change in government policies, market trends, etc. and to devise new strategies to stay ahead.
- To discuss new plans to induct new machines, training and concepts.
- Special meetings to discuss new projects and diversification plans.
- To assess and analyse projects/studies finalised and submitted by specifically constituted teams or task forces.

It may seem difficult to predict the length of a discussion but still you must fix timings and ensure to abide by the schedule. Open-ended meetings generally drift and spill over, both in course and time. Discussions tend to encroach into the available time. You must stipulate a time for the meeting to end so that everyone knows, and everyone can plan the rest of his or her day with certainty. Value of time must be highlighted in a simple but effective way stating beforehand, "This is what we have to achieve; this is the time within which we have to get it done." Of course, allocation of time should be reasonable to allow useful contribution by all concerned.

CONDUCTING THE PROCEEDINGS

Make sure that the meeting opens with professional solemnity and the discussion is launched as per the plan of the agenda. You may be conducting the meeting while being in the Chair yourself or a colleague/subordinate may be conducting the proceedings with you present to give the final decision on complex and contentious issues, if any.

To derive maximum advantages from the meeting, liberal and free communication should be facilitated as follows:

- Reiterate and emphasise the purpose of the meeting, the time allowed, and the norms to be observed by everyone.
- The co-ordinator or rapporteur of the meeting should take down notes throughout the proceedings. A summary of the consensus reached or decisions taken should be read out to all, item by item, on the agenda.
- The discussion will have to be moderated, controlled and refocused from time to time to keep the meeting on track as per the planned agenda.
- Criticism of a proposal should not be accepted unless supported by better alternative proposals.
- Likewise, projection of problems must carry suggested solutions too.

MATCHING METHOD WITH PURPOSE

The agenda of the meeting may suggest a particular way of conducting the proceedings. The method may vary in view of the type of items on the agenda or the purpose of the meeting itself. For instance:

- If the purpose is to *convey information*, the meeting might begin with a formal presentation followed by questions.

- If the purpose is to *seek information,* the meeting could start with a short statement of the topic/problem and then those intimately concerned with it may submit progress reports and explain the issues required to be highlighted.
- If the purpose is to *reach a decision,* the meeting might review the background, terms of reference and options available. The criteria to be applied can then be established to facilitate a decision.
- If the purpose of the meeting is to *introduce a change* — material, structural or conceptual, the meeting could take the form of a presentation by a subject expert or it could be a brain-storming session.

Whenever in a dilemma, ask yourself: 'What is the purpose of the meeting?' After getting the aim and purpose of the meeting clear in your mind, ask yourself: 'How can it be best achieved?' Your commonsense will then suggest a working method for effectively conducting the meeting. You just have to deliberately pause and think. Give a direction to the meeting and the meeting will work.

Insist on Preparation, Be Open to Ideas

The success of a meeting often depends on the confidence and preparation with which the individuals participate. Thus, all ideas should be welcome, even if sometimes an idea looks absurd. In other words, even not so attractive ideas should be treated seriously. It could be that a good idea has been misunderstood and would be lost if rejected merely on its face value. If people are made to feel stupid for submitting a naïve idea, you may never get to discover the best ideas of all.

For days on end, the Egyptian Army Engineers and Generals could not decide on the best method to flatten the near vertical sand-wall on the enemy-held bank of Suez Canal in the 1973 Yom Kippur War. It was operationally expedient to achieve this because the Russian bridging equipment (PMP) was to span the Suez, over which the tanks were to cross the Suez Canal and fight the Israeli army right through the formidable Barlev Line. It was, surprisingly, a naïve idea from a young subaltern that solved the most serious crisis of that moment. What could not be achieved by preponderant artillery bombardment and all possible demolition techniques, was achieved by water jets as suggested by the youngest of them, whose idea was initially pooh-poohed by the senior brains.

Avoid direct criticism of any person. For instance, if someone has not come prepared, he/she is bound to get exposed and his/her fault would become obvious to all. If you leave the criticism as being simply implicit in the peer pressure, your diffused disapproval and rebuke would be clearly understood by him/her and it will be for good effect too. If you explicitly rebuke and humiliate that person, it may embarrass the person too much and portray you as a sadist. Sometimes sterner rebukes are better conveyed by a sheer quiet look and body language than can be conveyed through words. Also, your position carries more dignity and awe if you practise tolerance and professional focus in dealing with individuals in public. Wilkins has said, "It is an excellent rule to be observed in all discussions that men should give soft words and hard arguments; that they should not so much strive to silence or vex, as to convince their opponents."

Responding to Problems

Here I offer some ideas on how to deal with various problems associated with the volatile world of meetings. Most of the problems in a meeting are best undertaken by the designated Chair; but sometimes, it is more appropriate and effective if another authority, directly concerned with the issues involved, responds to the problem with a suggested solution or decision. It may even be more prudent if the tricky, sticky problems are first tackled by a subordinate authority. You may ask, why? Because the proceedings will provide you an insight into the real dimension of the problem and you shall be in a position to find a better course of action to solve it. By trying out a solution through another authority, you get the option to adopt the most advantageous stance. To change positions or stance once adopted becomes embarrassing quite often. More senior the position, more difficult it would be to change your declared stand. It is always easier to vindicate and salvage your colleagues and subordinates than to rescue yourself from messing up a meeting.

Your reply will be very crucial in the event of any tricky issues surfacing. Sometimes prohibiting a discussion on such issues may give rise to speculation and rumour that might later on demand your attention even more seriously. Mature handling of queries is therefore crucial. Colton advises us, "Reply with wit to gravity, and with gravity to wit. Make a full concession to your adversary; give him every credit for the arguments you know you can answer, and slur over those you feel you cannot. But above all, if he has the privilege of making his reply, take special care that the strongest thing you have to urge, be the last."

Some of the problems can be nipped in the bud if you take note of the following points:

- When a participant strays from the agenda item, put him back on the track: "We'll deal with that separately, but at the moment we want to focus on a particular issue."
- If there is confusion, seek clarification: "Do I understand correctly that ... ?"
- If the speaker begins to ramble, wait until a little pause and jump in: "Yes, let's see if we got you right. Does anyone have anything to say on it?"
- If someone raises a controversial issue, refuse to discuss it: "We'll first discuss that in detail in my office; not here as yet."
- In the event of a confrontation taking place, try to diffuse it: "You can put down all your points in writing and bring them over to me. We'll discuss all that separately. At the moment we'll stick to the agenda and proceed further."
- If you find someone dozing or not interested in the proceedings, arouse him/her by saying: "What are your views on this point, Sudhir?"
- If a point is too woolly or too vague, ask for greater clarity: "What exactly do you have in mind; let's have more specific details on it?"
- If someone interrupts, you should suggest : "We'll listen to your idea after Mr Sharma has finished."
- If people chat, you might diplomatically and yet pointedly stop them by suggesting: "I think Mr Rao and Shalini, have something important to say. Yeah, Shalini, you have a suggestion to make?"
- If someone grimaces or gestures disagreement with the speaker, then make sure they are brought into the discussion: "What do you think about it, Mohan?"

- If you do not understand, say so: "I'm sorry, I do not understand that; would you explain it a little more?"
- If there is an error, look for a good point first: "I see the advantages of this point; but what if...?"
- If you disagree, be very specific: "I'm afraid I disagree because ..."

HANDLING CRITICISM AND RUMOURS

"Nobody listens here", "Look at him; he's taking sides", "The company is not doing what we want", "She's too moody", "The boss is assuming too much," are some of the refrains usually heard in cafes and corridors. People avoid saying openly how they feel because they fear offending others, or that it may cost them their job, friendship or goodwill. Such complaints or criticisms, if left unresolved for long, become too intense and an emotive issue to talk about. Holding on to unexpressed feelings such as fear, anger, resentment, irritation, despair or annoyance can aggravate the situation, with the negative feelings making inroads into a larger number of employees. If individuals fail to reconcile on these issues, then the pent-up feelings may end in uncontrolled outbursts of emotions, severe depression or physical illness.

People often use insulting and offensive language to express their inner emotions. People are bound to react to the insults. If the purpose of criticism is to make them think on what they're doing, and correct the wrong, then you need to respect their self-esteem. Knocking them down will be counter-productive and generate a defensive reaction.

Abstinence from criticism does not mean you have to accept

substandard work and indiscipline. As a manager and supervisory authority, it is your duty to ensure the highest standards of efficiency and discipline in the organisation. Questioning what is questionable, rejecting the unacceptable and rectifying the wrong is your job. But the way you do it is more important. Admonishing and rewarding are essential management functions. While rewards have better effects with wider publicity, admonishing should be discreet and calculated. For achieving better effect, here are some tips:

- Do it in private.
- Be specific and state facts.
- Think and decide what results you want to achieve.
- Criticise the conduct, not the personality.
- Be open-minded — have no preconceived ideas.
- Use a friendly approach; be a coach, not a hangman:
    1. Establish the facts.
    2. State how you feel, or the consequences, if the activity continues.
    3. State how you want it to be different.
    4. Get a commitment.

How do you face and react to criticism yourself? When we are criticised, we react in different ways, depending on our personality — either we refute ("never..."); defend ("but you see..."); retaliate immediately ("How dare you..."); avenge ("I'll show you..."); be obstinate ("Why? I will!"); jeer and sneer ("Oh! You will now educate me!"); withdraw quietly or sulk.

It is more constructive to develop an assertive response. Listen to what changes people want you to make; ignore the criticism. Consider the circumstances or the context and resort to humour, as it helps to put things in a light perspective. Alfred E. Smith has said, "Be sincere. Be simple in words, manners and gestures. Amuse as well as instruct. If you can make a man laugh, you can make him think and make him like and believe you." With this backdrop, it would be simpler to handle criticism too.

- Repeat clearly but coolly the words of the criticism.
- Ask for clarification (it gives you time to calm down).
- Deliberate over it without permitting vendetta to take over.
- Decide to agree or disagree.
- Humour and wit can be very effective, if carefully used.
- If you agree, acknowledge and announce what you plan to do to improve.
- If you disagree, do it tactfully. Develop logic and tact to convince people that criticism has been unjustified, unfair or exaggerated. Patience, reason and tact can convert others' harsh feelings in your favour. Anger and revenge will only justify the criticism and confound matters.

There is a similarity between armies confronting each other and two opponents trying to score a point over the other in social and professional dealings. In military operations, the weaker side makes great noise and kicks up dust to camouflage its own weaknesses. And the Army making such a show of force has, almost in all cases, no intention to really launch its offensive in that area. The real intention is to divert attention from something more sinister in the offing elsewhere.

PRESENTATIONS

Presentation is a pre-planned and structured speech for communicating information or ideas to a group of people in order to inform and persuade them on the intended strategy or concept.

It would normally involve suggestions, recommendations or may even raise new questions that would be food for thought to involve all in a common pursuit. Depending upon the nature and applicability of the subject, a presentation may be interwoven into a meeting itself so as to allow a detailed discussion on the concepts and ideas presented, and thus evolve a consensus.

No presentation will achieve its desired aim unless the presenter leads the audience through the following four stages smoothly:

- The audience must be able to hear you clearly and see what you have to *show* them.
- They must *understand* what you are saying.
- The test of desired effect on the audience is their *acceptance* of what they have heard.
- It must *motivate* them to initiate and sustain action in accordance with the declared objectives.

It is important to make your presentation last in the audience's mind because, as per some researchers, people forget: 30 per cent in 48 hours, 65 per cent in a week, and 75 per cent in a month! Thus, the final retention is 25 per cent after a month, unless their minds have been impacted in a more effective manner than through the usual lectures and instructions. That is why presentations are different from routine lectures or discussions.

We perceive happenings in the world around us through our five senses — some, of course, may even possess the sixth. When we involve more than one sense, we enhance the chances of comprehension and retention. For example, it is always easier to reproduce a story from the movie that you have watched only once than from the book you have read. Why? Because in the first instance, you *saw* and *heard*, whereas in the second you only *read*. Your experiences, where more of your senses were at work, are so deeply embedded in your memory that its essence remains there forever unless someone suffers from an attack of amnesia. No structured education teaches any child the taste of a chocolate. You remember it from the day you first taste one. The reason is that all your senses are at work at the first instance; you could *see* it, *touch* it, *taste* it, *smell* its aroma, and if not the chocolate itself, you could *hear* your sibling call for it. And since that day onwards you don't need to see it; your tongue tells you that it is the same delicious chocolate you ate that day with your sibling and how both of you fought over it.

If, therefore, you can make the audience take your presentation as a feast of ideas or concepts, they are likely to carry with them, not only the memory of what you presented, but would even nourish their own ideas with the intellectual delectation you gave them. You can do it with a little thought and preparation.

Preparation

What is the purpose of your presentation? Think over the requirements assigned to you. Discuss and find out if there are any terms of reference, restrictions or parameters within which you have to work and give the presentation. There can be restrictions of time, location and resources or equipment that you can hire or purchase. There can be terms of reference that you will need to highlight in your presentation, but which call for prior preparation. This exploration and preparation will enable you to clearly focus on the requirements.

Collect the literature you need, study it and prepare your draft presentation. Discuss your draft presentation with your friends. Take their ideas and questions seriously and find explanations to their queries during your preparatory period. Time permitting, discuss your requirements and preparation with experts on the subject.

As a guideline, your draft presentation should be at least one-and-a-half times more than the time allotted to you to present. When you have done this much, consider how you could involve the audience still more deeply as to enable them to enjoy and retain maximum substance of the message you convey. Technological advancements in acoustics, visuals and multimedia aids have placed a vast range of aids at your disposal. You can choose what you want and design your presentation in the most effective manner. You can choose what suits you to enhance the effect of your delivery. Do not choose too complicated an equipment as you may not be able to integrate it smoothly into your presentation.

Slides, LCD/laptops, audio-visual clips, demonstrations, short and crisp action plays help in conveying ideas more effectively. Innovative integration of interactive themes like games and quizzes makes the presentation even more interesting.

REHEARSALS

Some people feel that since they handle the subject daily and know all about it, it would be enough to prepare a slide or two and blabber for the forty minutes allocated to get rid of the responsibility. If getting rid of the responsibility is the aim, then it is fine; nothing else is required to be done. Even those one or two slides, in that case, are a waste. But if your aim is to put up a performance, then collect all the information yourself and help others to gain from the presentation, taking care to rehearse beforehand. If feasible, get some colleagues to oversee your rehearsals. Encourage them to ask you questions; seek their suggestions to hone your presentation.

Remember your draft presentation was one-and-a-half times longer than the time allotted to you! Now is the time to refine it here and there. Cut out the verbosity; trim it of the extra words and sentences; tighten the text to make it crisp. Your discerning mind will come to the fore to suggest how to reword certain expressions to make the presentation succinct, direct and pointed. Invite the maximum number of questions from your friends during these rehearsals. You will be glad when the audience too repeats these very questions.

For those who believe rehearsals are for novices, I have an experience to share here. I once went to the Rashtrapati Bhawan to meet a friend who was posted at the President's Secretariat. I had to wait for over two hours before he showed up. I was pleasantly amused when he told me that he was busy attending the President's rehearsal of his Republic Day speech to the nation. And, as he told me, the President (a man of unusual intellectual excellence — name withheld in deference to the highest national office) even invited suggestions from the small audience. And yes, a suggestion was made — even to the President of India!

Churchill's oratory inspires speakers even today. It is said he never made any major speech without making notes and rehearsing it.

THE PRESENTATION PROPER

Now having been through rehearsals, suggestions, deletions, additions and editing, your presentation must have acquired a shape, which should comprise the following:

- **Introduction:** Tell the audience what you will tell them through your presentation. It is the first and most important aspect of your presentation. How you launch the topic is significant for success of the subsequent voyage. You can think of an innovative introduction, i.e. a well thought out pre-rehearsed attention-catcher, an anecdote, a joke or an eloquent quotation. Once you have the attention of the audience, strike a friendly chord through comforting queries, like, "Can you hear me out there please?" or "I welcome you all to...and hope those of you who have travelled long distances to reach here are comfortable..." Light questions and interactive pleasantries at the initial stage help in building up a rapport with the audience. Then state the theme of your presentation and the proposed plan you intend to follow. You, perhaps, would have divided your presentation in phases or parts, each explaining the various segments of the presentation. Along with this scheme, also convey that at the end of the presentation, you would be fielding questions from the audience.
- **Main body:** This is the stage where you tell what you actually want to tell. The subject matter should be so organised that your message flows straight into the minds of the audience. Your language, style of presentation and aids

must simplify the presentation so that the audience comprehends what you say. To make the talk effective, the building up of the idea should be progressive and sequential. Develop an interactive approach to proceed on the presentation. Technological advancement has placed a large number of apparatus at our disposal whereby high quality presentations are no longer a problem. Utilisation of slides, audio-visual/LCD and multi-media aids greatly facilitate assimilation of information. The following points must be considered for generating and maintaining the interest of the audience:

- Highlight the newly emerging situation or requirement that has necessitated the presentation.
- What does the presentation seek to change?
- What benefits will accrue to people and the organisation once the proposals being advanced through this presentation are implemented?
- Will there be any change in the quality of life of the members?
- Prove any models of the proposals already tried out anywhere else and feedback, if any.

- **Peroration:** Now tell them what you told them through your presentation. Here you sum up all that you have explained, like reiterating the theme, summarising the main points and concluding the presentation with an impact. Impact can be created by ending your talk with a powerful and appropriate quotation, caution, or even a challenge thrown at the audience to incite them into a commitment.

At the end of the presentation, it is desirable to evaluate your performance by obtaining feedback from the audience. This feedback may be direct or indirect. In direct feedback you circulate a questionnaire or a simple card seeking brief comments, questions and suggestions. Indirect feedback is always available during informal chat at tea or lunch at the end of the presentation. Opinions so discreetly obtained are more objective and useful for improvement in future.

Communication is the nerve centre of all management functions, nay, human existence. Can we think of optimal relationships to grow and thrive in the absence of communication? No business, no transaction is possible without proper communication. With time at premium for professionals as well as families, shorter, crisper, pointed and effective methods of transacting ideas is the need of the day. That is why even individually we need to plan, organise, hone and present our ideas, theories and recommendations to the target audience to achieve the desired effects.

There is no alternative talent or system that can adequately compensate for lack of communication in the world. People have to share views to develop their relationships and personality. In modern times when no one seems to have time to listen to details, effective communication has acquired greater significance. It is to separate gossip from information and knowledge that structured communication in the form of interactive sessions, meetings and presentations has grown and proved effective. Even unorganised conversations during tea intervals, social gatherings or informal or casual chats in the corridors and cafés leave an impact on people's minds, if carefully done.

Public Speaking

It is by speaking that you influence, control and direct people. It is a very significant tool to project your personality. It is not possible to penetrate others' minds and know what lies hidden there. Learning public-speaking techniques is therefore very important for enhancing personal effectiveness. And, of course, we learn to speak by speaking.

Public speaking is an essential attribute of leadership. There are numerous leadership traits and qualities, but no single leader has them all. Oratory, however, is one such quality without which no leader can become a mass communicator. Obviously, it is this quality, which is common to all leaders at all times.

How can we empower ourselves with the ability of effective public speaking? Since many aspects of inter-communication in general have been discussed at length in the previous chapter as well as in this one, I will briefly but specifically delineate your road-map to great performances in public speaking.

Important Guidelines

- **Mannerism:** As a cardinal doctrine, remember, you speak with your whole body: your face, eyes, your shoulders, hands, etc. Some stand and remain stationary at the lectern. But then there are those who move about on the stage — some even through the audience — and you have different impressions about each of them. You can try out your own style by standing in front of the mirror and try to adopt gestures, body movements, facial expressions that suit you best. Take the help of your friends. Most important: Be natural, as artificially put-on acts betray you in the eyes of those watching every move of yours.
- **Clarity:** Get in command of your ideas. Line them up in a sequential, logical order. You must be clear of what you are

talking. One idea explained is better than ten poorly delivered. There are techniques to aid your memory. You may keep a small pocket-sized card with salient points sequentially noted thereon to help you remain on course through the speech; you may devise your own technique to link one point to the next and so on.

- **Appeal to feelings:** Abstract words cannot be pictured and are therefore difficult to comprehend in the right context. Use of examples, comparisons, picture words and simple vocabulary are found to be effective in moving the audience. For example, words like *'sacrifice, labour and grief'* may convey your broad meaning but don't you feel the effect would be vastly different and touching if the following words were used instead: *'blood, sweat and tears'* ? Therefore, say 'Honda City' not 'car'; 'Osama bin Laden', not 'a mad fundamentalist'; 'a second Mother Teresa', and not use 'a very kind and generous lady.'
- **Road-map:** Your speech is like undertaking a journey. Where are you heading — the audience, your co-travellers want to know. So, organise your speech in a manner that you 'tell them what you'll tell; then tell and tell what you told them.' To cite an example: "In this talk of mine today, friends, I would like to tell about the increasing menace of terrorism facing us today: its genesis, the states most affected by it, losses in terms of lives and material suffered so far, its future dangers and, lastly, some recommendations to contain this menace."
- **Audience involvement:** There are some common faults some speakers commit: poor eye contact (looking in the blank or at the ceiling), stony face (no cheer, zeal or eagerness — repulsive looks), no emphasis on key words,

use of pedantic homilies and harangues. Nobody in the audience likes to be treated like a school kid. So, it is necessary that you involve the audience, take them along mentally with you by exchanging reassuring looks, nods, questions and opinions.

How to Begin a Speech?

A good start is the key to the success of the rest of the speech. You have to, therefore, plan and rehearse the introductory part of the speech very thoughtfully. Here are some hints for an influential start:

- **Capture the attention of the audience:** Actual incidents, experiences briefly mentioned prove useful in getting every-one to listen to you. Give them a slice of life — real life experiences — that can amuse, startle, or shock the listeners when thoughtfully woven into the speech. For example: "Yesterday when I was giving a talk on 'Parenting and Personality Development', at Turning Point India, a lady intervened to say, 'I was born without parents and yet'..."
- **Stimulate curiosity:** If you tickle and trigger their imagina-tion, people will remain attentive and eager to hear more. For example: "It is an alignment of too many celestial bodies in one line. Next fortnight, when they exactly come on this line, it will be catastrophic. The earth will be sucked away from the Sun and life will come to an end in a moment. Watch out; we all have just 15 days more." Or it could be a more positive and pleasant start: "The man who did the first ever space walk and walked over the Moon, will be here tomorrow along with Miss Universe for an informal discussion session and lunch with you."
- **Dramatise facts and statistics:** Like plain faces do not

attract much attention, plain language, facts and statistics too do not matter much unless spiced with attractive wrappings of language, voice and gestures. For example: "Fifty innocent human lives, thirty of them women, many children in their tender years — age eight and below, three in the wombs of their mothers yet to see this world, were burnt sleeping in a train compartment for no other reason than believing in a God different from that of the brutal killers. How different? Nobody has seen, no one knows."

- **Ask a question:** There are innumerable unasked and unanswered questions in public mind. When you ask the same questions, you stir up their interiors and they get hooked to you. For example: "Do you know what takes to succeed like Bill Gates?" or "Do you know why the corrupt politicians in India never get convicted?"
- **Display technique:** If possible, have something that you can show to the audience — it could be articles or papers that add a punch to your comment. For example: "Who says it can't be done? Here it is, right here (wave the relevant papers); these are the letters of confirmation. They have done it..."
- **Identify with the audience:** Wear a friendly look, cheer and smile. From your voice and gestures too your friendliness should drip. Exchange glances, smiles with inquisitive faces in the audience. It is not feasible to give you an example here on this point. Practise grimaces in the mirror.
- **Theme reminders:** Convey the central idea of your speech early and in concise form. As you progress through your speech, repeat the theme occasionally to remind the audience and get them back on the track. For example: "Countries that cannot defeat terrorism are losing precious lives

and will, one day, lose their freedom too."

- **Use examples, comparisons:** Picture words, stories, examples, comparisons and experiences remain in the consciousness quickly and stay longer in memory. For example: "American role in the Indo-Pak dispute is like the proverbial monkey mediating between two cats fighting over a *chapati*..."

Focus 3: Put Your Communication Skills to Effective Use!

- No communication is complete unless some one *listens* to you. Attract *listening;* it can't be compelled.
- It is not only through your lips and words that you communicate; your whole body communicates. Mirror exercises can help.
- Make people internally experience what you are saying. Touch their feelings.
- Involve the audience in your thought process by seeking approval, confirming a statement by asking them leading questions or even quoting some common experiences shared by most of them.
- If the audience is not buying your idea, it is not that your idea is poor. For centuries, we have believed we were descendants of God. Darwin dared to speak up and the entire enlightened modern world today agrees with his irreverent theory that monkeys are our ancestors!
- Accessories like your voice, non-verbal language, mannerisms and orchestration of presentation are more important than your words to cast the desired effect on the audience.
- Get to know what the listener expects. Your talk must contribute and seem to satiate the aspirations of your audience in some manner.

(*Contd.*)

- If you have organised your presentation with forethought, it would echo in your audience's ideas. This will ensure their instant support to your ideas.
- Let the hardware accessories (equipment, acoustics, lighting, visuals, etc.) not distract attention. These are to accentuate the impact of your talk; not to hamper listening.
- Let them feel that you are speaking what is in their minds, and you will dominate their minds!

HOW TO CONCLUDE YOUR SPEECH?

When the main matter of your speech is over, pause and repeat the theme once again verly slowly to emphasise the point. Then, if you had started with a quotation or a story in the beginning, go back to it and connect the theme to it.

Have a rehearsed one-liner ready to cast a solid impact of your speech on the minds of the listeners so that it continues resonating in their ears, until much after you have finished. It could be a quotation relevant to the main theme, a snippet or a short proverb.

SPECIFIC ACTION PLAN

A - Possession of refined communication skills is an asset. Where can you use your newly acquired or enriched communication skills for tangible gains? Write down your answers in point form here.

____

____

____

____

____

____

B - What preparations does this venture require and how do you plan to go about it?

C - Choose at least one occasion this month in your office when you will present at least one proposal for improvement in ... (*your wish*). Prepare and present it.

D - Visit the institute/school/college where you were a student. Interact with the Principal/Director and the staff. Keep such interaction with intellectuals alive. Volunteer to contribute and share your professional knowledge with them. Mention hereunder the names of institutions and intellectuals/professionals you plan to visit/meet within this month:

E - Be on the lookout for workshops/seminars, and attend as many as feasible. Then share your experiences with your friends.

The souls of men of undecided and feeble purpose
are the graveyards of good intentions.

— Anon

4

Problem Solving

The more important you are, the more you are busy solving problems and making decisions. Since childhood all of us have been solving problems by reacting to them in certain ways. Young managers are under the gun — stressed and bereft of time. Consequently, when they encounter a new problem or a situation that demands decision, they react by groping through certain templates that seem to them to have worked well before. It is easy to adopt this approach whenever you are caught in the intriguing swirl of solving the same problem over and over repeatedly. Therefore, as a new manager, you'd better get used to an organised and systematic method of *problem solving* and *decision making*. No situation repeats itself. There can be no fixed prescription or template that can be mechanically applied to solve problems and arrive at the right decisions. There is a need for innovation, creativity and the capacity to take risks.

Here I offer you some guidelines that will perhaps prepare you with the much-needed wherewithals to deal with the problems that crop up and call for workable decisions in time — a dire need of the day in all occupations today. Ponder over it and, if possible, create mock situations with limited participants to test these guidelines a few times over. Remember, decision making is essentially a leadership function and therefore responsibility, accountability and risk factors are inseparably linked with the process of decision making. Big decisions mean big responsibility, bigger accountability and even bigger risks! If you do not wish to take risks, you may not be able to take decisions. If you do, your decisions may lack objectivity and may result in multiplying the problem. It is simple: If you run away from a problem, it chases you. If you start confronting the problem methodically and boldly, you will find not only solutions, but will discover that most problems soon transform themselves into opportunities.

There must have been moments in life when you faced situations, which you thought were serious problems, like exams, interviews and competitions. But when you took them as a challenge and came through successfully, you realised they were the stepping stones for moving further on in life. Those who treated these opportunities as problems, buckled and ran away discovered that they had not actually run away from problems; they had actually run away from opportunities to facing problems. Subsequently too, when you did get the job, you came across cranky bosses, argumentative subordinates and deadlines — all vexing problems. When you learnt to deal with the bosses and subordinates and developed your efficiency to meet the given deadlines, you found these very problem-like situations becoming your planks for leaping forward.

That is also why people charged with drive and determination view problems as opportunities. What a strange phenomenon that most mothers consider giving birth to a child, which they so desperately desire, as a big *problem* too! Doesn't it give enough insight into our misplaced notion about life and our gross misconception about the terms 'problem' and 'opportunity'?

Of course, it is not to suggest that everything in life is hunky-dory and opportunities rain from heavens to give happiness, success, health, prosperity and fame in the world. There will be problems and you will be required to be tough and strong to face them. If you have faith in yourself and in your Creator, then take it for granted that no problem in this world can be more powerful than your potential to overcome it. Only you will have to decide first whether you want to solve the problem squarely or whether you want to run away from it. If you face it now, you might uncover and find some dream opportunities hidden in it. If you choose to avoid it, it will chase you and harass you for long.

Is there a method in solving problems? Of course, there is. As a matter of fact, it is the neglect of methodical ways to deal with things in life that gets us into problems. Let us think of a system that will simplify our approach to problems and help us in finding effective and timely solutions.

IDENTIFYING THE PROBLEM

This is where people mostly err and struggle. They react on their initial perception of the problem and on what appears to be a problem even before collecting the necessary inputs. Thus, in a way, they are not addressing the problem proper; they are addressing what they think to be a problem. So, a game of shadow-boxing begins. After doing quite a few rounds of fighting the silhouette, you get exhausted while the opponent is still fresh and fighting fit. You cannot get to the target until you identify and fix your sights on it clearly. The same is true of our personal as well as professional problems.

Therefore, you have to understand more about why you think there is a problem. Often, as you would experience, it is the small things like a hinge, pivot, swivel or fulcrum that provide a meaning to bigger things. This is precisely so with humans too. Seek answers to your smaller questions of life and you will start doing right things in life soon. John Forster has very aptly said, "It is a poor and disgraceful thing not to be able to reply, with some degree of certainty, to the simple questions, 'What will you be?' or 'What will you do?'"

STEP 1: WHAT, WHERE, HOW, WHEN, WHOM AND WHY!

Seek answers to the following questions; you may co-opt others to assist you in this exercise:

- What exactly is it that makes you think that it is a problem?
- Where is it happening?
- How is it happening?
- When is it happening?
- With whom is it happening? (*Caution:* Don't give in to the temptation of jumping to 'Who is causing the problem?' Go for issues; not people. This will ensure objectivity in your approach.)
- Why is it happening?

- Write down the identification of the problem in brief description. This description may be something like: 'The following should be happening, but it is not happening...' or 'The following is happening whereas… should be happening.' Be specific in your description. If you have found the answers to what, where, how, with whom and why, it is happening, then it will be easier for you to be specific.

STEP 2: ONION PEALING

Your answers to questions listed in Step 1 above will sometimes result in new discoveries. You may find numerous minor problems wrapped up in the main problem. This may distract you and dissipate your time, resources and energy, if not carefully sifted. Complex problems will always have their roots and branches spread out to areas out of your main focus. Therefore, it is prudent as well as expedient to break it down into tiny parts through the process of onion pealing. This process involves repeating the process of answering questions given in Step 1 above, until you obtain descriptions of several related problems.

STEP 3: VERIFICATION

Don't be impatient to issue a directive or take a decision immediately. Speedy decisions can be hasty decisions. You must be clearer by now in your mind. The problem must have started crystallising into some shape. You are now having a clearer image of things and better understanding of the problem. But all you have is the outline of the problem. You have to dig a little more.

By the time you arrive at this stage, you are in a better position to discuss and debate your problem with friends, colleagues, experts and professionals. You would have gathered inputs that have made you more focused on the subject. You are no longer groping in the darkness. But still, there is scope for more inputs. What lies in the areas not explored by you? You have viewed and analysed the problem from your angle. Now, if you brain-storm the inputs collected so far with your confidants and experts, you will enlighten yourself in three ways:

- If you were objective enough in your analysis, you will receive an endorsement of your understanding of and approach to the problem. This will provide you the very much needed (and deserved too!) confidence that will prepare you better to deal with the problem.
- New inputs from others will prevent you from taking wrong decisions and help you in identifying the so-far-unseen aspects of the problem.
- This process of verification through brain-storming will provide the early indications of the possible fallouts of certain actions being contemplated by you. These spinoffs or fallouts may be either advantageous or disadvantageous. In any case, you will be wiser before acting.

Step 4: Prioritise the Problems

When you discover that you have several related problems facing you at the same time, you must prioritise which one to address first. While allotting priorities, you must classify various problems according to their importance and urgency. As a rule, urgent problems require immediate solution. These problems may not be too complex in the beginning, but if left unattended, may acquire serious ramifications. Cases like electrocution in the assembly line due to faulty power supply system; complaints of molestation of a teacher by the Principal; failure of machine/ equipment or strike by workers when large orders gasp for immediate supplies, are some of the problems that require urgent solutions. Problems like slow-down in productivity; falling profits; workers' training in view of intended modernisation; increasing absenteeism; waste control, etc. are important to be solved but there is no emergency calling for immediate action. For emergencies and urgent problems, you cannot indulge in prolonged discussions, analyses and comprehensive policy formulations, which are very desirable for finding lasting solutions and are important, but not urgent.

Such is also the case in personal life as well — we have urgent problems and important problems that need action. A thief breaking into the house can heighten the urgency to an alarming level of emergency that warrants immediate action. In such an event, your actions are triggered more by reflexes and intuition because the situation does not permit detailed planning. But tackling the thief alone was the urgent problem. The ineffective security system in your premises that facilitated the thief's entry is yet another problem which is important.

Sometimes, what we consider to be important are really just urgent problems. Important problems deserve more attention. For example, if you are mostly busy answering urgent phone calls, then you probably have a more important problem — developing a mechanism whereby your phone calls can be screened and prioritised.

STEP 5: UNDERSTAND YOUR ROLE IN THE PROBLEM

Your role in the problem can greatly influence the course of the problem and its solution. In situations where you are directly responsible and authorised to deal with the problem at hand, you should exhaust your ideas and efforts in finding the right solution. But jumping into another's problem with superficial understanding of the problem and throwing in comments or ideas casually can be counter-productive. Remember the advice, *'All of us ought to swap problems because we all know exactly how to solve the other person's problem.'*

In dealing with organisational problems, your position, terms of reference, organisational interests, will delineate your role fairly clearly. There will be occasions, however, where you would be co-opted in dealing with problems and decision-making mechanisms. Your involvement may be sought because of your expertise or experience. You may be placed on the decision-making body either because of your seniority or because of the likelihood of the problem or decision impacting you or your department in some way.

Your role will have a meaning if you see the problem in its real dimension and feel (not think) the need for a pragmatic solution. This will be possible if you play your stakes and interests involved therein. Wherever this is not so, contribution from outside is most likely to be perfunctory, sometimes even misleading.

FIX THE CAUSE

An exercise through the above process would be to delineate a fairly distinct profile of the problem by now. To establish the cause or causes of the problem, it will be often useful to collect opinions of other individuals — one at a time, because some people tend to be inhibited in the presence of others. It would help you immensely to write down your own brief notes concerning the problem as you go through the above process.

Now take down what you have heard from others. Collection of others' views is particularly important where the problem is performance related.

Now, when you compare your own notes with the assorted views of people you consulted, you can fix the cause of the problem in an unambiguous statement of the cause. This statement must answer the following questions:

- What is happening?
- Where is it actually happening?
- When and how did it commence?
- Does it serve anybody's interests, if it remains status quo?
- Whom is it affecting most?
- Why is it happening?

ANALYSE ALTERNATIVES AVAILABLE

At some stage you have to decide whether to co-opt others in your approach to resolve the problem or do it all by yourself. More often than not, it is useful to keep others involved unless you are facing a personal problem. Even personal problems can be better resolved if you have a confidant who is concerned and competent. For finding effective and lasting solutions to personal problems, a candid and dispassionate introspection opens up new vistas and alternatives. If you do not wish to share your secrets with anyone, then you will have to debate and sift the issues with yourself. When we say 'yes' and 'no' together in the same breath, there are two different entities of you debating the issue. Don't get vexed by this dilemma whenever it occurs. The conflict within is actually a battle between the finer virtues vibrating in you and the malevolence or mere passivity preventing you from changing the status quo. This too is an internal brain-storming and, if alternatives are freely analysed in terms of advantages and disadvantages of each, the exercise often results in providing new and useful solutions.

For professional problems a brain-storming session is required. Since the resolution of the problem is likely to affect others, brain-storming will help you in collecting and screening as many ideas as possible to choose from. Remember not to pass any judgement on the quality or relevance of the ideas expressed while collecting them. Just write them down as you hear them. Encourage people to come out with whatever they have in their minds. After exhausting idea seeking, commence evaluation of ideas so collected. Efficacy vis-à-vis advantages and disadvantages of each must be analysed. It should be clearer and easier for you by now to grade the ideas in a preferential order.

At the end of your analysis of alternatives carried through brain-storming, you will have a very clear view of the options available.

SELECT THE BEST OPTION

When selecting the best option, again view the problem in its entirety. Have a *helicopter vision* that enables you to survey the whole expanse and not a *tunnel vision* that confines your approach to a narrow lane. Then consider:

- Which option is most advantageous in the long term?
- Which option is most realistic to accomplish?
- What resources, if any, are required to put the best option into effect?

- Do you have enough time to implement the option?
- Are there any side issues or likely fall-outs which need to be addressed simultaneously?

FINALISE YOUR ACTION PLAN

- Carefully consider the post-solution scenario: 'What will it be like when the problem is finally solved?'
- Consider what specific steps should be taken to implement the best option.
- Mull over on what systems or processes should be changed in your organisation. You may need a change in policy or procedures too.
- Devise a mechanism to monitor the implementation of your Action Plan.
- Does your Action Plan need additional resources in terms of people, money and facilities?
- Set deadlines; anything that is not time-bound cannot be fully accomplished. Monitor progress regularly and fix a date by which you would like it to be accomplished.
- Demarcate responsibilities for implementation of the plan. Those who are responsible must be accountable too.

MONITOR IMPLEMENTATION

Ensure timely inflow of feedback along with the progress of implementation. Merely expecting the results will not make things happen; inspecting and monitoring will move things better. Some of the indicators to look for are:

- Are things moving the way you desire?
- Is the plan progressing as per schedule?
- Is there any aspect of the plan that requires a review?
- Are the resources being judiciously utilised to accomplish

the plan on schedule?

- Is there a need for revising the priorities that were initially allotted?
- Is there any change of responsibility required?
- Has the implementation given rise to fresh temporary problems that need to be taken care of simultaneously?
- Is any other mid-course change warranted?

INSTITUTE A COMPREHENSIVE FEEDBACK SYSTEM

Bigger problems are important and need a planned approach because they influence the future. If tackled in time, they will not acquire emergency dimensions; even their urgency may not be too expedient. When we talk of the emergency nature of the problem, we imply that the problem is erupting, or may even have erupted already, into a state of crisis. Effective feedback provides you a peep into the potential breeding grounds of problems whereby you can initiate timely precautionary actions.

Nevertheless, problems have a way of occurring in life — personal as well as professional — because status quo is not acceptable to individuals and organisations in forward gear. It is necessary to either change the state, conditions and circumstances or our approach to things around. Most of the problems knock at our door to remind about the need for change. They jolt us out of complacence and impending stagnation; they present new opportunities too. But new opportunities become apparent, depending upon the strategy we adopt to pre-empt or solve the problems.

If only we reflected sometimes, we would be amazed to realise how little we actually know about what we don't know.

Therefore, in this phase, it's critical to institute measures to obtain regular feedback in different ways. This is necessary not only to pre-empt the likely problems but also to be in tune with the current times and needs. This is a pro-active way to grow, evolve and remain in the lead.

To be of value, feedback must be assessed objectively, but then how to obtain the feedback? A few of the methods that have been tested and found useful are:

- **Formal reports:** Devise formats to collect views, comments, complaints, recommendations and alternative proposals, from people concerned. Do not discourage adverse comments and complaints at this stage. Analyse these and collate the substance of the feedback on a single paper. Study these observations at length through a process of '4Rs': *read, reflect, recall* and *review.* Then act on '4Ds': *deliberate, debate, devise and decide.*
- **Brain-storming sessions:** Don't hesitate to hold these sessions involving various categories of people, depending upon the nature of the subject/problem at hand. For deciding about the participants, choose those directly concerned with the problem; who are indirectly affected by it; and who can be in any other way interested in it. Remember, you are not yet seeking a final solution to the problem. You are merely allowing everyone to open out and express. Let the deliberations be free and frank. Make everyone feel that his/her point is important. Rules of the session should encourage participation but must not allow individual criticism. A senior moderator must ensure that it does not drift into a gossip session. Lying somewhere in between the ideas and comments you will find some very useful feedback that

will provide you a pathway to proceed further on.

- **Informal interactions:** Visits to the plant or sites give a fair idea about the way things are happening. Problems of equipment, work-environment, views, ideas and problems being faced or anticipated by the people provide a useful insight into the environmental realities and perceptions of people around. Informal chats over tea, away from the halo of authority, also provide the right environment to obtain a peep into people's minds and factors influencing them.
- **Casual activities:** There are some organisations which attach great significance to emotions of people. Employees in Sahara Group are not called *employees* — they are called *members* of the Sahara Parivar. How aptly someone has said, 'Give the people the belief that they govern and they will be governed.' Casual activities like picnics, sports, fun parties, family welfare activities, children welfare programmes, etc. sometimes throw up useful feedbacks for strengthening the organisations.
- **Indirect spinoffs:** Customer satisfaction, fluctuations in expenditure graphs, misinformation campaigns and even anonymous/pseudonymous threats by rivals and your own dissatisfied elements are early indicators of some brewing problems. Casual comments, complaints or even appreciatory views about your people and organisation could be indicative of how things are moving and what can be anticipated.

'SEARCH AND SOLVE' MISSIONS!

In times of war, the most daring and worthy missions are commando operations. These are *'search and destroy'* operations, which are launched by commandos on the nerve centres of the enemy's military power, deep inside the enemy territory.

Pre-emptive actions by these few hand-picked men often cripple the enemy's potential so seriously that the offensive, which would have otherwise required much larger formations of thousands of men with staggering cost in terms of life, material, territory and prestige, is nipped in the bud. Well planned and executed '*search and destroy*' missions open out new opportunities and more options for you to profit from. Why? Because the underlying principle on which these operations are based is '*hit the problem in its womb!*'

Do not allow the problem to grow. Look out and search for its breeding places. Past experiences, your own as well as those of your friends and even competitors, will enhance your sniffing power to smell problems in their inception stages. There are other methods which will further sharpen your skills to anticipate, trace and destroy (if that word is scary, call it solve!) it before it really becomes a problem. We will discuss some of these pre-emptive *search and solve* missions here now.

BRAIN-STORMING SESSIONS

A common mental weakness some people suffer from is their defeatist attitude, 'I am doomed. I can't find any good solution to this problem.' Nature, however, is a big teacher too. Such people spend most of their time brooding. Spurts of brighter ideas too, do flicker off and on, through their broodings sometimes. It is these flickers of positive ideas, which, if tapped and harnessed properly, can carry the person to the opposite extreme, i.e. create as many workable options as possible, each with varying degrees of usefulness in terms of cost, effort, time and ultimate advantages and disadvantages. If you expand these ideas and debate within your own mind, the result will be a revelation. This process of mind-churning, which is referred to as *atma-manthan* in Vedic teachings, pits your two inner selves — the positive and negative — against each other. The inner duel, if earnestly fought and candidly umpired by your conscious self, can provide worthwhile solutions.

In modern times, however, we have turned this exercise into a public activity in the form of 'brain-storming sessions', which afford us insight into others' minds as well. In place of a single brain, it is a multi-brain churning activity with each idea triggering another in another mind. Through such organised sessions, we can also gain knowledge from experts and experienced people. Those who are directly affected by the problem will be happy to be part of the solution-finding activity.

The success of the brain-storming sessions largely depends on adherence to the following principles:

- The more the ideas, the better it is. Let there be no limit on *wild* ideas, no matter how outrageous or impractical they seem.
- At this stage, *quantity* is more desirable than *quality*.
- No idea is absurd, ridiculous or bad. Hence, no criticism of any idea should be allowed. You never know when excellence and genius lie hidden in an apparently silly idea. Newton's first idea too was derided by many intellectuals of that time, who later acknowledged the scientist's wisdom!
- Proliferation of ideas — building ideas on others' ideas — is encouraged.
- Everyone must be encouraged to contribute actively.
- Judgemental approach on the quality of the ideas offered during the sessions must be curbed, because judgement

inhibits imagination.

- Record every idea on a white board/flip chart. While recording, do not associate names of sponsors of these ideas.
- Select the best five ideas (combine similar ideas when required).
- Now rank the ideas individually.
- Decide, as a group, which idea is to be enacted first.
- Begin the brain-storming process again as necessary.

This way you would have a pool of ideas. Let there be a tea-break after this and exhort the people to come out with even more ideas, if they so desire. The second stage of the brain-storming session starts after the break. Collect additional ideas (if any) within the next ten minutes or so. Then proceed to discuss and identify the most promising ideas. The process of elimination through discussion and on the basis of *inter se* merits of the ideas will bring into focus the most profitable options.

Whether it is in a group or alone, no idea should be overlooked. Make sure that you make your brief notes; new ideas evaporate rather fast. If faced with a tough problem, solutions will not come easily. It requires continuous training. In the Army, they play 'war games' when it is peace time. Why? Because a military leader must inculcate the habit to visualise battle situations, analyse all possible options, select the best course of action and plan his operation accordingly. When it is happy, relaxed days, spare a little time from holidaying and invest it in visualising and conceptualising contingencies. It is desirable for all responsible persons to practise generating solutions not only to simple problems, but, to impossible problems as well. Thinking big expands the capacity of the human mind to think of bigger and better solutions. Besides your own work, try to find answers to bigger problems; for example, national and international problems; municipality problems in your area; your neighbourhood problems; how poverty and illiteracy can be eradicated from the country; what can be a lasting solution to encroachments on government land — roads and parks, how to improve security and entertainment facilities in the colony, etc.

Such personal and group-level exercises will not only provide the right solutions to problems, but also significantly improve your own work-environment and expand your capacity to handle problems successfully at high, very high levels. Finally, it fosters your confidence in your ability to find effective solutions and being creative and able to cope well with complex problems in life.

Make it Your Baby

Last but not the least, decide where the buck must stop; never try to pass it on. If you want progress and development, you shall have to face problems. Never consider the problems tougher than your determination. There can be no problem in the world that has no solution. If you involve yourself deep enough in resolving the problem, there is no reason why you should not succeed. My friend Mansoor narrated a small story that he happened to hear somewhere during his treks. It highlights a very common reason why most people run away from difficulties, and abandon them half way.

There were two warring tribes in central Africa. One tribe had a dense forest as its domain, while the other tribe lived in the open plains. The jungle tribals lived on whatever the forest gave them and enjoyed hunting for their needs. They envied the plains-people who prospered through agriculture and trade in the more civilised world. The jungle tribe would often invade these farming families and take away their exploits. One day, as part of their plundering, they kidnapped an infant of one of the farming families and absconded with him into the forests.

The plains-people didn't know how to cut through the dense, inaccessible, thorny undergrowth. The danger of snakes and wild animals, besides the blood-sucking leeches, deterred them. Besides, the farmers had never ventured into these forests and had no knowledge of how to pick up trails to trace the abductors of the infant.

These problems notwithstanding, the farmers selected some of their toughest and bravest young men and sent them out into the jungle to search and bring the child back home.

The men debated and brain-stormed on various methods of cutting, clearing and making their way through the jungle. They first tried one method and then another. They tried one trail and then another. After several days of effort, however, they had cleared only several hundred yards. New problems were now emerging. 'We must arrange to carry water and supplies with us. What of the wild cats and snakes and leeches? We must carry enough medicines, deterrents and danger-warning systems.' Plans that were simple initially were now becoming complex and cumbersome.

Feeling hopeless and helpless, these tough men decided that the cause was lost, and they prepared to return to their village, out of the suffocating forest. As they were packing their gear for the exit, they saw the infant's mother emerging from the bushes in front. Bruised and cut all over, with her clothes almost torn into shreds, she heaved herself with the baby wrapped and tucked safely on her back, into the clearing these brave men had cut over days. Wonderstruck, they realised that she had penetrated the inaccessible forest and accomplished the mission all by herself, whereas they had not been able to make any headway.

Amazed and stunned, everyone watched her in disbelief. One of them dared to ask her, "We, the strongest and the ablest men of the village, couldn't get through this treacherous jungle, how did you do this all by yourself?"
She shrugged and said, "It wasn't your baby."

Make the problem your baby and you will not only tackle it successfully, but more speedily and effectively too!

My narration of this story should not lead anyone into the belief that one needs to steal others' problems mindlessly. Here too, you must ascertain your role in such problems, which may not concern you at all. Nevertheless, if your neighbour's house is on fire, it is not his problem alone. The fire, unless fought and put out, might engulf your house too. But there are people with incredible talents who dump their own problems on other people. Look around and see if anyone is using you as a garbage pit for his own problems. For instance, a couple whose marriage you had facilitated fell apart after a couple of years of the marriage and sought divorce. Both of them were determined to separate for good. It was neither your fault nor your problem. You didn't have to ruin your own happiness for such problems in which people directly concerned are not as upset as you find yourself. It would have been emotionally foolish. Of course, all you could have done was to render sincere advice and help wherever you felt socially or professionally responsible, morally bound or emotionally attached.

Problems cannot be always seen in a personal perspective. Problems affecting a group or organisation will have their share of effect on you too. You, therefore, have to discharge your part of the collective responsibility very sincerely, as in the case of your neighbour's house being on fire. Once you have accepted that you must act towards finding a solution to the problem, make it your baby — you will hit on the best solution!

Enrich Your Problem-solving Calibre

How do you feel after completing a hard day's work? You feel great and tell everyone who matters to you about your accomplishment very proudly. But you do not want people to know about your escapades if you spent time seeking carnal pleasures, sleeping, eating and doing nothing! When do people around you genuinely admire and feel proud of you? It is never because of your easy, lazy, extravagant and luxurious habits. It is one single quality that rallies people around you and marks the beginning of your journey to success — your capacity to accept challenges. This personality trait will not be found in people given to easy life to start with.

Pramod, a successful entrepreneur and an intellectually awakened friend of mine, summed up the entire gamut of problem solving this way: "Struggle is the toast of life. If you ever happen to spend a day without facing problems, you may be under the wrong impression that you are alive. If you did nothing to solve a problem and went to bed after an eventless day, then pick up the morning newspaper and check up its obituary columns — your photograph with a homage may be there!"

And *Rig Veda* endorses, 'It is the inner courage of decision making with unambiguous clarity of mind that distinguishes between the winner and the loser. It is not religion, caste or colour that classifies humans into categories. If that were so, they would be anatomically distinguishable. But it is not so. It is man himself who makes a decision to take up the challenge of problems whereby he would distinguish himself or perish like lesser mortals.'

> *Akshanvantah karnavantah sakhayo manojveshv asama babhuvah.*

(Men endowed with similar eyes and ears alike are unequal in their potential and resolve to confront and surmount odds/ problems).

— Rig Veda: 10/71/7

Every problem you solve makes you feel more confident, stronger and wiser in facing and solving future problems. Top jobs often entail nothing more than solving problems. It is therefore prudent — even expedient — that you should develop the habit of solving problems. Helping others in finding solutions to their problems will benefit you in two ways: firstly, it will earn you good friends; secondly, it will be an excellent experience that will sharpen your skills and boost your self-confidence. Of course, be careful not to trespass into somebody's protected territory while offering to help in problem solving. Also, don't allow yourself to be overwhelmed by emotions while offering help to others. Surcharged emotions tend to precipitate decisions without much thought, which is dangerous for both — you and your friend/relative.

BEWARE OF QUICK-FIX SOLUTIONS

Decide for yourself: do you want hasty, easy and cheap solutions or effective and lasting solutions to the problem? Since the former are the product of shortsightedness and not vision, they are seldom the best. Running away from a problem is by far the easiest 'solution' — if that were a solution — to some problems; but problems have a nasty habit of tracking us down. Drugs and alcohol can make you forget your problems for a while, but while that problem still remains, your easy solution is slowly nursing new problems. The hangover of problems lingering is far worse than the hangover of last evening's whisky.

If your solution to one problem gives rise to two more problems, it is not a solution. In the garb of a solution, you are actually buying a future problem. Develop a vision to view your tomorrow clearly. As someone has aptly said, 'Tomorrow is the day that comes just when we have figured out today's problems.' Let there be a dawn of wisdom that will lead you to effective and lasting solutions — not to cheap quick-fix solutions that work as manure for fresh problems.

BANISH PROCRASTINATION

In problem solving, I would like to recommend the most effective method: Please do it yesterday! Now, this proposal amuses you. Maybe you are laughing at the idea itself. But I laugh at the idea of those who say, 'I'll do it tomorrow.' There are only two days — yesterday and today— that you have seen, my friend. You lived through these two days and could not do it. You have not even seen the day for which you are postponing your today's burden. When it does come, tomorrow will become your today and again you will replay the same song: 'I'll do it tomorrow', until you abandon the thought of solving your problem. Yes, it happens to some people. They make problems a part of their lives and slowly learn to live with them. It is painful to see people treat problems as procedures and even solutions in themselves.

Smriti, a young IPS officer in UP cadre, was on a surprise inspection tour of police stations in Sitapur. Sitapur was a district that had earned the dubious distinction of being one of the top three, criminally-notorious districts of UP. As she stormed into a police station, the police personnel and the SHO scrambled for their uniforms and accoutrements, and were soon herded together before her. Instead of the staff, her attention was caught by a haggard, old woman sitting under a tree, in the courtyard. Smriti walked to her and was amused to discover that the woman was muttering to herself something.

"*Mataji, kya baat hai?* (Mother, what's the problem?)," Smriti enquired of the emaciated woman. From beneath her mangled leathery remains could be seen what must have been a charming human face, years ago.
"*Rapat nahin likh rahe*... (They are not recording my FIR)," the old woman sobbed, confiding that her young daughter had been abducted.

"Kya naam hai apka? (What is your name?)," Smriti tried to peer into the gasping hollowness of humanity.
"Gunvati Devi. *Pati ka naam* Puran Chand. *Chaar saal ho gaya daru pee ke mar gaya. Hamko rone ke liye chhor gaya...*" Gunvati Devi erupted and poured out in torrents. There was an ocean precariously kept compressed under a dry, parched outer crust, which was now bursting out.

Smriti turned and looked at the SHO who told her that the FIR had been duly recorded. He called for the official records which Smriti studied. He also told her that a police party was already out in search of the missing girl and her abductors.
"Your FIR has been recorded and the action to arrest the criminals and recover your daughter is already underway, Mataji. Why are you under the impression that your FIR is not recorded?" Smriti tried to explain to her in Hindi.
"No; I still say they have not recorded my *rapat* (complaint). I may be illiterate, but I know it costs Rs 200 to lodge an FIR. I offered this amount to Munshiji, then to Darogaji but they all refused," the relic of ancient wisdom reasoned.

Bemused at the woman's thinking process, Smriti felt sad and genuinely concerned for the old woman's missing daughter, who was safely recovered by evening the same day. She felt even more sad at the mindset of the people whom she and her force sought to serve.

In recording the FIR, her problem had met a solution but Gunvati thought the solution itself was a problem. It is conditioning of the mind. When you procrastinate, this is what finally happens. You succumb to the problems and make adjustments with whatever is around. When you accept problems as unavoidable, you tend to modify your behaviour to suit them and get accustomed to whatever the state is.

Gunvati was so conditioned and tempered by happenings in life that she strongly believed there was no such thing as free justice. And Gunvati is not alone; I have come across highly educated and well-to-do industrialists who get more worried if their gifts and favours, a commonly practised gesture in return for grant of permits, licences, etc. are declined by some scrupulous government officers. They have become so accustomed to the culture of corruption that they do not believe passports, licences, permits and other free privileges can be granted for free. So disoriented people's minds have become that absence of a problem becomes a problem — a scary problem at that!

All procrastinators take shelter under strange reasoning cunningly developed by them to escape from reality. Some find the popular adage that has become an oft-repeated cliché, 'time is a big healer' very handy in fooling themselves and others. Time may be a healer for the finished past, but not for live and active problems. Problems have another stark reality: they do not die of old age. Unfortunately, every passing day makes a problem stronger than yesterday. With more time, each problem develops a potential to breed more problems.

That an innocuously easy-going habit like procrastination can seep to such depths and concretise itself so firmly among individuals must be treated as a serious social and national malaise. Certain traits can degenerate the entire character of individuals and thereby multiply cumulatively to become a social psyche of the order described above.

The resolve and determination of individuals is a source of their power. Those who lack it are dominated by others — even weaker and less gifted. In Vedas there are repeated exhortations asking humans to decide, move and act without wavering and losing precious time. In the *Gita* when Lord Krishna exhorts Arjuna to decide and focus singularly on his duty, Arjuna realises the significance of making a resolve to dare even the most daunting of problems frontally.

Generations of physically strong people have been subjugated by the weak for no other reason, but due to lack of courage to face problems and make decisions to move on. Slaves obsequiously served their rulers for centuries until one of them decided to rule. And lo behold, how he ruled; he paved the way for a slave dynasty to rule a mighty nation like India. It is not ridiculous, nor humiliating; it is revealing and inspiring.

Devaasa aayanparanshoorvibhranvanaa vrishchanto abhi vidbhirayan.
Ni sudravam dadhato vakshanaasu yatraa kripeetamanu taddahanti.

(Come forward, you the people who are confident and strong; arm and equip yourselves with requisite accessories, go right through, removing dense forests. Prevent and change the course of rivers if they be obstacles in your way. Surmount all odds and annihilate the hostile forces and set them ablaze).

— Rig Veda: 10.28.8

CONFIRMATION

Solution of problems provides immense satisfaction. The solution itself is the reward to your effort. You will experience it when you do it. But what is the confirmation that the problem has finally been solved and not put off to a distant future? Resumption of routine operations with perceptible renewed zeal

Focus 4: There's a Solution for Every Problem!

- Problems do not die of old age; they grow stronger with time. In the early stages they can be solved or dissolved sooner.
- Take a *helicopter view* of the problem. Discard *tunnel vision* to understand the depth and spread of the problem.
- Prevention is better than cure; it is true of problems too. Keep vigil and act in time.
- Most problems are transparent — some partially opaque but none is wholly opaque. If you peer through them a little harder, you will find both: causes and solutions.
- Opportunities never come as gifts packed in glitter and colour and addressed to you by name. They are always disguised and concealed — mostly in various shapes and hues of problems.
- Regular inflow of feedback, informal inspections/visits and interaction at all levels can provide early warnings on potential problems.
- Take a long-term view of the problem. It will erupt again out of patchwork solutions.
- Remember, any problem that has not killed you will make you stronger once you solve it. And you are very much there — stronger too!
- Ensure accountability and institute definite measures against recurrence.
- Your own mistakes will teach you well; learn lessons from others' mistakes too.

and mutual co-ordination is a sure confirmation of the fact that your problem has been finally resolved. But it is not yet party time for you. It is time to consider what changes should be effected to avoid the eruption of such a problem in future. Changes may be required in policies, procedures, training and administrative functioning.

It is very useful to write down the lessons learnt as a result of this problem solving. Share it with your supervisors, peers and subordinates. Sharing the lessons even with your counterparts in other organisations may be mutually rewarding in future. Every problem thus resolved would make you wiser, stronger and more competent as a manager and leader.

The way you look at a problem is very important. It shows your success potential and is a sure indicator of how you will fare in life as a leader. Whatever be the problem, the first thing to do is to assume that there is an answer to every problem. And the answer is in your reach; it just needs to be discovered. Worrying is neither thinking nor exploring; it is debilitating, it is negative thinking that pushes you further from the answer.

Specific Action Plan

A - Briefly write down the worst two problems you have faced in life and solved so far.

____

____

____

____

____

____

B - Mention the two main strategies, methods or techniques you adopted to solve these problems.

C- What is it now that is holding you back from doing what you wish to do in life? State your problem in absolute, clear terms.

D - What makes you feel that you may not be able to solve your problem?

E - Think of an occasion when you advised and helped your friend or relative to wrestle and come out of a problem. What do you expect from others and why?

F - Make a list of concrete actions you plan to take to solve the identified problems from today onwards and go ahead resolutely. You are bound to win!

"Aoum! Ayutoahamayuto ma aatmaayutam ye chaksharyutam me shrotramayuto

Mei praanoayuto mei apaanoayuto mei vyaanoayutoaham sarvam."

"Aoum! Devasya twaa savituh prasaveashvinorbaahubhyaam puushno

hastobhyaam prasuut aa rabhe."

—Atharva Veda: 19/51/1-2

(I am endowed with thousands of Powers. My Aataman, my body, my heart and mind, my eyes, ears - all organs and faculties - are endowed with infinite energy and potential. Each breath I inhale and exhale, the vibrancy of life in me - my entire being is empowered with infinite potential and invincible verve. So, gifted with these powers (that are unique to Man in the animal kingdom) with your inspiration, Oh! God! I take decisions and initiate action with patience, determination and supportive elements at my command.)

5

Decision-Making

What is life? Is it not a series of decisions, howsoever minor or major? If you do not live your life through decision making, then you are either already dead, or in some deep trance or at best a domesticated animal in a herd of cattle which has to be told what to do and what not to do. It is through rational decisions that we take charge of our lives. It is the cumulative effect of millions of decisions we continually take in our daily activities that determines the shape of our lives. But these are those decisions which come easily to us because of our continuing experiences in life. We treat these as trivial not because they really are so, but because we have acquired the confidence and competence to deal with them, even if they happen to be hazardous. Man has converted so many dangerous activities into adventure and sport. Not too long ago, the initial decision to launch oneself in activities like skydiving or hang-gliding was wrought with extreme danger; today we crave to experience the thrill and our decision is not only spontaneous, but we are prepared to pay for it too.

Sometimes, even decisions having long-term effects on our lives are greatly influenced by emotions and enthusiasm, which may evaporate over time. The new realities can create a shift in one's inclination and decision-making mechanism. This may cause either a total reversal of the earlier decision or its modification to suit new requirements, that either were not visible or had appeared too trivial at the outset. Lt Atul Mahajan's case explains all this in detail:

Fervour of pure patriotism and courage inflames the youth whenever their country faces a challenge. The Kargil war in 1999 ignited this fervour in Atul Mahajan too. Born in an affluent business family in Delhi, he decided to join the Indian Army while in the final year of MBA, much against the wishes of his parents. He was commissioned into the Punjab Regiment in June 2001. His battalion was deployed at a hot spot of military activity along the Line of Control in Jammu & Kashmir. While on his way to his assigned post in the forward area, Lt Atul Mahajan encountered heavy enemy shelling that was quite a common occurrence whenever the Pakistanis observed any movement on the Indian side. Atul's escorts advised him to rush to the communication trench in front. While scampering into the trench, Atul saw one arm of the porter accompanying them sever and fly off, even as a lot of dust and rubble came and settled over them. The porter was attended to immediately by the soldiers who were quick in administering first-aid and finally evacuating him to the medical-aid post.

This was a shocking experience for Atul who had heard but never seen such a ghastly scene with his eyes so far. Too stunned and dazed, he could not eat or talk for hours. He did not have the heart to venture out of the trench. Atul reminisced how his parents had advised him against the profession. Cursing himself for his foolish decision to join the Army, he toyed with the idea of quitting. Even as the shelling continued intermittently, Atul saw men laughing, joking and moving around, as though nothing untoward had happened. Atul, wrapped in the cumbersome bullet-proof jacket and helmet, could not sleep although the night passed silently.

On the field telephone, Atul tried to sound normal but the tremor in his speech betrayed his feelings as he gave the okay report to Major Dahiya, the company Commander. Major Dahiya said he would visit Atul's post next morning and have breakfast with him. Lt Atul Mahajan, accoutred in bullet-proof jacket and helmet, received his company Commander at the minefield entry point. He had arranged for breakfast inside his bunker. Major Dahiya, however, ordered it at the View Point, where he would brief the subaltern about the defences, battle procedures, enemy activities and other tactical and administrative matters. Major Dahiya, dressed in his tracksuit, had, like any other day, come on a run. No escorts, no weapons — a shockingly casual way to move around in an active battlefield! But for Dahiya, such casual behaviour notwithstanding, symbolised courage and commitment from which his men drew inspiration.

Sitting on campstools in the open, he chatted with Atul over a frugal breakfast. Suddenly there were several blasts with the clatter of machine-gun fire following. Atul dived into the nearest trench; but there was no more fire for the time being.

"Where is this fire coming from? Can you spot which post of theirs is it? Take a pair of binoculars and see if you can..." Dahiya thought he was talking to Atul, but Atul was nowhere to be seen.

Atul peeped up to find his company Commander still busy eating his toast and tea, out there in the open — unperturbed and unmoved, even after such hell had rained over them. Atul thought Dahiya must be mad.

"Here, I will show you some important enemy locations....Where are you Atul?"
"Lt Saab *kahan hain*?" he asked the nearest soldier.
"Sir, Yes Sir...I'm here, Sir," Atul's voice croaked from the trench below.
"Are you okay? Any problem?"
"No Sir...er, yes Sir, I am okay."
"What the hell are you doing there in that bloody ditch? Come here, I'll show you where it is coming from..."

Atul came up. As they stood surveying the Pakistani posts with their binoculars, another barrage of machine-gun fire and artillery fire started. Atul tried to dash to safety again but found himself held from the straps of his jacket by Major Dahiya.
"Son, you will have to see if you want to stop it. Come on, stand up and look in the front," Dahiya patiently but firmly advised the uninitiated subaltern.

Once the source of fire was spotted, Major Dahiya was quick to decide mounting a decisive fire assault on the errant enemy post. His further orders brought hell on the enemy bunkers. Atul saw them crumble under intense fire, with smoke and flames billowing high into the sky. The fire assault continued for about two hours and virtually destroyed the forward elements of the enemy.

Atul realised that he had sprained his ankle while jumping to safety. His earlobe too had suffered a cut when it got sandwiched between his carbine and the edge of the helmet, during his scamper to safety. He had not realised the injury until then because its pain had been hidden under fear. As he realised that Dahiya's methods were surer ways to achieve safety, he felt pretty foolish. He soon discarded his bullet-proof jacket and helmet and decided never to go down to save himself from enemy fire. Timidity soon gave way to pride, personal safety to dare, and confusion to decisiveness. Atul felt guilty for the temporary cowardice that had overwhelmed him even as he saw Major Dahiya unfazed and unmindful of the danger that had pushed him into the trench on the reverse slope. The leadership in him was now triggered by his company Commander's personal example.

Not only did Atul face the future enemy firing with dauntless courage, but also planned and led a daring raid on the enemy post that was applauded by all his subordinates and superiors.

This story highlights the following aspects that often influence our decision making:

- **Emotional pulls and pressures:** As a student, Atul read newspapers, watched TV channels reporting from the battle-front and heard tales of valour. The surcharged atmosphere in the youth motivated him and he instantly fell for the adventurous life in a military profession. No analysis and logic advanced by his parents and relatives in favour of a business career made any sense to him. He became so imbued with the idea that he would not listen to anything against serving the Army from anyone. Army, Army, and only Army — 'nothing else for me', he thought valiantly. Kargil possessed him. So, he made a decision to join the Army. Academically brilliant, he easily qualified the Union Public Service Commission (UPSC) examination and was selected for commission in the Army.

- **Risk factor:** Risks involved in the Army life were explained — even exaggerated — to him by his parents and relatives. But Atul boldly brushed their arguments aside. This was easier to do at home because he was not yet face-to-face with the risk and danger. Once he came face-to-face with the dangerous realities at his forward post in J&K, he nearly succumbed and quietly decided to quit the dangerous life. He was suddenly repentant of his earlier decision to join the Army and for defying his parents' advice. If his earlier decision to join the Army was impulsive due to heightened emotions of patriotism, his decision now to quit was no less short-sighted, resulting as it was from panic.
- **Initial perception of the situation:** Initial perception of the situation can create false pictures in the mind. Misled by these images, people often make erroneous decisions. Atul's initial perception of the battlefield was more like the depiction in action movies that make most people feel small for not having become soldiers. Atul was understandably moved to take a manly decision. The situation where he

found himself under fire was dreary and he thought he was doomed. Such extreme misinterpretations of the reality are, of course, momentary. Decisions made under pressure or fear continue haunting people concerned, who repent for succumbing and relenting too early. Atul had already decided to quit. He would have given effect to his decision had he not met Major Dahiya under those trying circumstances.

- **Intellect:** Understanding the situation in its true perspective is necessary. Dispassionate examination of the situation and reviewing your opinion helps in removing all misgivings. Atul's encounter with Major Dahiya changed his initial perception of the situation. What followed thereafter was a virtual transformation that he underwent. In one casual chat over breakfast, even while the bombs and bullets rained all around, Dahiya's composure and unruffled countenance so boosted Atul's morale that the soldier in him surged. He felt so guilty of harbouring fear and making a cowardly decision to quit that he not only banished the idea of quitting the Army, but even desisted from wearing the bullet-proof jacket and helmet.

It is so funny and yet so common that some of the most important decisions in life, such as education, career choice, marriage, etc. are often impulsively or casually made. People jump to conclusions and decide on serious matters of life without much deliberation and thought. Love at first sight, euphoria at the first job or cases like Atul's desire to run for safety are witnessed almost daily by us. As a contrast, some relatively insignificant decisions, such as the selection of a shirt or trouser, or colour of bathtub, or the type of table at a restaurant are reached after considerable survey, debate and deliberation. Is it a case of misplaced priorities or lack of concern about important things in life?

Human beings have conscious and sub-conscious decision-making abilities. We respond to certain emergencies even before we realise the actual nature of the emergency. For instance, the speed at which we withdraw our hand at the touch of a needle or an electric shock is unusual, when we never really move our limbs at that speed. The leg of a sleeping person seems to automatically decide and pull out instantly from a pinprick given to arouse him. The harmony in human body and mind provides immense agility and decision-making prowess through reflexes. But such decisions are only to save us from immediate danger. It is a defensive and reactive mechanism, which is not enough to shape the course of our lives. For permanent removal of the danger, we have to consider various factors and decide on some definite course of action. Such decisions cannot be left to reflexes or whims.

Behaviour scientists often emphasise the significance of cognitive processes of generating creative ideas, collecting specialist opinions, assessing the probable outcome of each alternative, etc. to develop a sound decision-making mechanism. However, when too much caution is applied in decision making, the process slows down, resulting in loss of valuable time and perhaps even dissipation of resources too. On the other hand, when too much swiftness is applied at the cost of relevant factors, there is the danger of a crash. These dilemmas are often compounded by some barriers to sound decision making, some of which are:

- **Impatience:** Impatience will often impel you to jump to a conclusion. It also hampers your search for relevant data. Here one feels keen to reject uncomfortable inputs in a hurry to decide. Premonitions surround such impatient people and they do not want to see the details beyond their nearest point.

- **Lack of self-confidence:** The consequences of feeling inadequate, dependent, or scared are obvious. You will not take any decision or allow yourself to be lifted and carried by the next wave. A very dangerous situation indeed!
- **Emotional swings:** The right approach to a situation is sometimes blurred and diverted by restrictions imposed by one's desire to be admired, credited, and so on. This can result in either the right decision or wrong, depending upon the source of motivation. The danger of a shift from the focus and emotional pitfalls is, however, very real in this case.
- **Unreasonable dependence on data:** Inputs are necessary in decision making. But arming yourself with cent per cent inputs is hardly, if ever, feasible. It would be something like a titular president functioning in a parliamentary democracy, where cent per cent complete work is brought before him for his signatures, for which he is not even answerable. In real life, you cannot abdicate responsibility for your own decisions. It is more like the presidential form of government where the Head of State takes risks and owns responsibility for the decisions taken.

When Lee Iacocca was creating history in industrial management by making novel and daring decisions that changed the fortunes of two car-manufacturing companies — first, Ford Motors and later, Chrysler Motors, some friends — all Harvard graduates and senior managers in other companies — asked him all about the secret of his success.

"We work so very hard in carrying out market surveys, studying new developments, collecting 100 per cent accurate data, debating proposals and strategies at length before coming to any decision. And yet, we find our decisions not achieving half of what you seem to be achieving," one of them grumbled.

"The trouble with you guys is that you went to Harvard," Iacocca chuckled, as he took a dig at them.

"What do you mean?" one of the friends took offence at this derisive remark.

"Yeah, I mean it," Iacocca insisted. "There they unfortunately teach you to first collect cent per cent inputs and then make a decision. The problem is that nearly 80 per cent of the inputs are already available. What you are doing is that you do not want to take a chance and invest valuable time and resources to collect the remaining 20 per cent inputs. What actually happens is that by the time you have pooled in these 20 per cent inputs, the previously available 80 per cent data become outdated. So you see, as a matter of fact, you are basing your decisions only on 20 per cent inputs that are current and relevant. The rest of your 80 per cent is no longer true. In my case, I think it is worth taking a risk on 20 per cent and decide on where you are 80 per cent sure already," Iacocca explained very plainly and candidly.

MECHANICS OF SOUND DECISION MAKING

GRAB THE OPPORTUNITY

A situation well understood and clearly stated simplifies decision making to a large degree. The gamut of decision is not limited only to problem solving or crisis management. Most of the decision making is about taking charge of life and steering it ahead. It would be sad if we treat every available opportunity as a problem. People must devise proper mechanisms to initiate action in a pro-active manner rather than wait for a situation to develop to force them into taking a decision.

In fact, most of the problems in life occur because we fail to take the right decision at the first opportunity. Life is just another name of action. Action is the product of decision. Without decision it is impossible to act. These are ways to keep us going so that whenever we stop, we are reminded to act, to move on by occurrences, called 'problems'. An opportunity not treated well becomes a problem. We must therefore respect opportunities. We must wake up when an opportunity knocks at our door and welcome it. Even if we miss it, it will visit us again, perhaps now disguised as a problem. If we run away, then the problem will chase us. When we face it, it has a way to revert to its previous form, i.e. as an opportunity that will carry us to success.

Whenever we are uneasy in life, it is not always because of problems. Unless clear about the existence of a problem, we may be uneasy merely due to inaction and indecision. Rather than thinking rationally and initiating desirable actions, some people start worrying. They do not know what actually they are worrying about. Worry then starts acquiring shapes of illusions and hallucinations. This happens to people who spend time and energy worrying about something that never happens. They actually need to make things happen. For this there is no alternative to coming to a decision and moving in some direction.

Asking yourself the question will help clear the mist: 'Am I exaggerating or underestimating the problem?' If you strongly believe there is a problem before you, then try going through the steps suggested in the previous chapter. If in doubt, it is better to open out and consult friends and professionals. Never entertain sinister thoughts that push you towards pessimism. There is always a way out of the present predicament. If you are facing the worst ever times, remember that nothing worse can now happen to you. You are poised only to emerge out of it to see better times. But if you indeed are in such a dark hole, you have to move to come out of it.

Greed may also cripple your decision-making ability. There goes a story that is not new, but it explains this rather simply. A woman went to Chandni Chowk, one of the oldest markets known for haggling, in Delhi. The woman, though new to Delhi, had been briefed and warned on the importance of haggling while shopping in such places.

"Show me an umbrella, please," she said, on venturing into one of the busy shops that had spilled over, far on to the pavement outside. She was shown a number of umbrellas out of which she selected one.
"What will it cost?" She dared to ask while fortifying herself against the impending pillage attempts by the shopkeeper.
"Rs 100 only, ma'am," announced the shopkeeper.
"Sorry, that's too much. I can't give you anything more than Rs 50 for it."
"That's too less for it. But early in the morning (it was 2.00 in the afternoon then), *bohni ke* time (harbinger of profits), you can take it for 50."

"How stupid of me, I should have said Rs. 30..." muttered the woman to herself, cursing her generosity that allowed the shopkeeper to make inroads into her purse. She suspected him to be making a huge profit by cheating her. "No, no. I'm sorry, fifty also is too much for this small fragile umbrella. Anything more than Rs 20 would be unreasonable for it..." she whined.

"Ma'am, where will you get an umbrella for Rs 20? But since it is *bohni* time, we won't like you to walk away without it from here. Well...take it for Rs 20, if that has to be so..." the shopkeeper grumbled.

'They can't be so generous. He still must be making a lot of profit,' the woman quietly reasoned within herself.

"Sorry, others are selling it even cheaper..." she said, before walking away. She was now confused and could not make a decision. When she started walking out, the shopkeeper made an offer: "Okay, Madam. You need not pay even Rs 20. Please take it for free, but don't walk away like that."

'There must be something fishy in this offer too. I only hope, I'm not cheated,'—the woman's greed was in conflict with her caution. Finally, greed emerged the victor! "Alright; but I want two," the woman responded.

This is what happens when you drift from your aims and objectives. A clear understanding of your real requirements gets blurred in the shadow of greed and caution. Not only do you lose direction of your journey, but also earn rebuke and ridicule that destroys your self-confidence as well as reputation. Swaying between two options also lowers the quality of your decisions.

Design Your Own Future

Decision making presupposes courage to accept a challenge and risk. This is what makes the real difference between victory and defeat. Vedic literature is replete with exhortations to humans to decide and move into action — for that alone is life. When Lord Krishna preaches the Vedic wisdom through the *Gita*, he goads Arjuna to make a decision and act with resolve without being drawn towards allurements *(aasakti)* or worry at the outcome of pure, sincere effort *(karma)*. A message in *Atharva Veda* too highlights the power of decision making. The key to good fortune lies in the decision. In fact, life in the absence of decision making would be a mere human wreckage. Vedic philosophy inspires man to carve out his own future. When you dare and decide, everything you aspire for falls within your reach. But you have to unlock the door to move in!

Dandah shaasti prajaah sarvaah danda evaabhirakshati.
Dandah supteshu jaagartti dandam dharmam vidurbudhaah.

(*Dandah* (baton) symbolises the authority to decide. One who has the power to make decision can alone rule the masses. It is this power of decision making that can provide all-round protection. It is the decision that awakens people. Righteous people deem this ability to make decision as *dharma*).

— Manusmriti: 7/18

The fact that you are reading this book shows you are concerned about your career. A decision about higher studies or choice of career delineates the future course of your life and you find yourself going in a particular direction. Obviously, your aim in life is critical here. Sit down and reflect on what you actually want in life. Consider all possible questions seriously:

- Do you want to make lots of money and possess all material luxuries of life?

- Or, do you want a satisfying job where you can put your expertise to use and achieve professional excellence?
- Or, would you derive more pleasure in an activity in which you help others and alleviate their problems?
- Are status and social acclaim more important than money to you?
- Are you willing to work sixty to seventy hours a week with no time to yourself, your family or your friends and relatives?
- Are money, status, and material allurements a sure way to health and happiness?

Different jobs offer different benefits. There isn't a profession where there is universal satisfaction or happiness. You can find happy and unhappy people in the same profession and organisation despite similarity of pay, perquisites and service conditions. To be happy and contented, it is essential to do a job you love. There have been numerous cases of frustrated cine-stars, industrialists, politicians, bureaucrats and military generals running amok and committing suicide. Their money, status and authority — all combined, failed to give them happiness. Consider the following hard facts:

- Shortage of money may cause problems but abundance of it does not guarantee end of problems.
- Being jobless can be a serious hardship, but being employed is not a guarantee for job satisfaction.
- Poor diet may sometimes be a cause of malnutrition, but rich food is a sure cause of obesity and complex health problems.
- Money and position can afford you the best doctors and medical care, but cannot guarantee perfect health or longevity.

- Your status and position can get you the most beautiful/handsome spouse but that does not guarantee you happiness.
- You can have bungalow, car and exotic luxuries at your feet, but that too may not guarantee complete satisfaction and happiness.

It is therefore necessary to introspect and find out what exactly you want in life. The value system you champion, your abilities and aptitude will guide to focus correctly and look for the right openings. Once you are determined to excel in your chosen field, you will not need even an 'opening' — you will burst into success by the sheer dint of the strength of your determination and perseverance.

Once you have decided on a philosophy of life, most other decisions will fall in line. What should be your future like? Visualise and try to see yourself ten years hence. There may be compulsions to join an intermediate career and shift to your real choice subsequently. Let your mind figure out what you need to reach your goal and how to prepare yourself for it. Allocate priorities to your needs and choices. Money, health, family, children, friends, socialising, work and so on should be considered to clearly fix their relativity and relevance in day-to-day life. Individual needs like privacy, comfort, status, health, education, hobbies, games and sports, entertainment too are important aspects of life and must be given their due place. This will help you come to the right decisions. If you have no priorities, you will not be able to decide where to go in life and which route to take.

You can't become a doctor, engineer, lawyer, manager, and

psychologist — all combined in one. Nobody can. Those who have known success are not known for their excellence in every field. They are known for one field of excellence only. In medical profession, it is not the specialist who attends to all kinds of ailments; it is the one with lowest qualification who does so. It may be the kindergarten school teacher who dabbles in all subjects of her class, but at higher levels teachers specialise only in one subject at a time. Never aim at being Jack of all trades, for if you do so, you will never be a master of anything. When you narrow down your options, your attention and efforts become focused. Look into the future. Laser-fix your aim as pointedly as Arjuna did. He could see only the eye of the pigeon — the point of his aim — not the tree, its branches, other birds or even the rest of the pigeon itself. Arjuna's aim was narrow, sharp and straight like a laser beam. Such pointed concentration will surely hit the target.

Get rid of self-doubt and avoid thinking in terms of either, or, e.g. either I will be an engineer or a doctor; either I will marry Shweta or someone else; either I will buy a car or I'll commute as hitherto, and so on. If you think like this, you are dissipating your energy and dreaming potential. Imagine yourself making out a cheque like the one below:

Pay________________ self or my wife ________________
Rupees__either one thousand or two thousand. Rs 1000/- or 2000/-

We know pretty well what will happen to this cheque. Ambiguous desires, expectations, dreams and aims will meet the same fate. There is, therefore, a need for us to put a check on this kind of wasteful thinking. You will start seeing specifics when you get clear and crisp answers to questions like: *what, why, where, when* and *how*. It will help further to think on these questions and demand specific answers on a daily basis, as an exercise to refashion your thinking.

When you have done this, your mind will comprehend the design and be able to visualise the exact shape of your future clearly. You will then have a visible goal to achieve. It is important to see the future you want, for you cannot achieve anything until it is visible and perceptible. You have to decide *now* what you want.

One Step at a Time!

Patience and perseverance are the basic essentials to keep you on the right track. Remember, 'a thousand-mile journey starts but with one step'. But you cannot start from the destination; just as a child cannot start his or her education from say, matriculation, skipping the primary and middle classes. It is the law of Nature. We grow in life step by step. Right from birth, a child grows systematically to cover different stages of progress in life. A child feeds on mother's milk to start with; then gradually learns to drink from a glass or dish. Toddling to walking; drooling to talking; education to jobs; playing to leading — every step is significant in one's progressive growth. What can you skip from infancy to childhood, to boyhood to manhood? Imagine what would happen if a student chooses to skip alphabets and wants to learn grammar to begin with on his first day to the school. Or an excited young painter, with no idea about boxing, suddenly decides to compete in a state-level boxing tournament without going through a progressive schedule of training. The result of such decisions will be disastrous. It is not so because of the cruelty of destiny we so easily tend to blame; it is impatience that prompts us to take a short cut to success.

Imagine a curious setting. A farmer's family is in need of some money and food-grains. He walks up to his fields, sprinkles some wheat grains as seeds and engages harvesters to reap his dream of yesterday. How funny, you would say. He will not even find sprouts in the furrows so soon! The farmer has to prepare his fields first by rigorous and repeated ploughings. Then he must treat the soil for the crop he wants. He must select the best variety of wheat as seed. He will be required to water his fields, sow wheat, and prepare furrows and channels for subsequent watering of the crop. As the crop grows, he sprays insecticides and fertilisers to protect it and enrich the crop in quality. From time to time he does weeding and watering. Then only can he expect to harvest a good crop. He can skip the steps in this process only to his own detriment.

The same is true of human growth. You have to make a start from where you are today. Treat each step you take forward as a miniature objective in itself. Congratulate yourself for your progressive achievements on each step. This will give you continuing satisfaction with inherent motivation. There will be several intermediate objectives to be achieved before you reach your final objective. It will need a series of decisions, which you will have to evaluate and review from time to time. Start taking small decisions with a clear idea about what you want to do to achieve the perceptible objective. You will progressively find it simpler to take major decisions too. Such is the process of your evolution to expanding horizons of success.

OVERCOME EMOTIONAL BARRIERS

The following barriers to good decision making may arise, which we hardly, if ever, figure out:

- **Excessive caution:** Decision making is a prerogative, power, responsibility and risk — all at the same time. But there is a peculiarity here. While you can be insured against the most serious risks of life like accidents, injuries, diseases and even death, there is no insurance cover anywhere in the world to protect you from poor decision making. This makes some people withdraw from the adventures of life — accepting things as they are. They feel resigned to Fate and put their life on an auto-pilot without any navigational aid. And some even disguise their apprehensions and brush away opportunities by saying, 'Why should I bother, it is okay as it is now.' Some others feel defeated even before starting, 'I don't think it is possible for me.' Whatever way you feel, it is your decision — floating and browsing around until you crash one day. Do you want to lead this kind of a life?
- **Personal problems:** People have their own personal problems that curb decision making. For instance, attitudes like anxiety, depression, dejection, feeling of being worthless — all these depend upon the degree or intensity of the problem one suffers from. They need proper psychiatric treatment, as mental disorders interfere with decisions and may even lead to self-defeating acts, which can be as serious as suicide or other crimes.
- **Conceit and ego:** A bloated ego and exaggerated notion of oneself too blinds one against the reality. It creates a screen between him/her and the situation. Decisions influenced by conceit and personal hang-ups can be disastrous. In 1980, Bill Gates, President of Microsoft, offered his computer operating system to IBM. A team of IBM executives considered his offer and rejected it. This was a decision influenced by conceit and ego. As was subsequently realised, this was

the "worst business decision of all time". An international giant, IBM soon paid the price for this mistake. When obsessed with the power and position you occupy, or when you make a move *to* teach someone a lesson rather than considering the merits of the case in a win-win situation, the dangers of such disastrous decisions become grave.

- **Surreal ambitions:** While some people, because of their negative disposition, feel *'kuchh nahin ho sakta…'* ('nothing can be done...'), there is another group which believes in wishful thinking in many forms. There are people who demand nothing short of perfectionism. There are yet others who want simple solutions to all problems. Some, in hurry, want it all their way or all for themselves only, apprehending things will get worse sooner or later. The idea of too much too soon can look magical and very tempting, but then you are gambling. Of course, ambitions must have challenge as an essential ingredient to drive you, but care should be taken not to cross the precincts of reality and pragmatism in defining ambitions. All these surreal expectations clutter up one's thinking and make a mess of decision making.
- **Absence of review:** Occasionally, when we look back over the mistakes we made and how we could have done better, we receive useful feedback. There will often be scope for mid-course correction where you can modify your decision and plans. Regular monitoring of the progress can prevent things from going downhill. Periodical review will not only help in regaining control of the situation, but also in enriching your decision-making ability and self-confidence.
- **Impulsive decisions:** Emergency situations can force us into taking prompt decisions. But these decisions must be

short term, with inherent flexibility to change and adapt to emerging environments. Impulsive decisions, however, are different from emergency decisions. In emergency decisions, it is the situation that warrants immediate decision. In impulsive decisions, it is the decision itself that is dangerous and is most likely to engender problems. Impulsive decisions sometimes become mad decisions too. Imagine a situation where a minor row between a husband and wife ends in filing a divorce suit. In another case, a BMW owner whips out a revolver and shoots at another car just because the latter did not give him the space to pass on the road. For right decisions, there is always time; for impulsive decisions, there is no time.

Most of these emotional barriers are passive forces that hold people back without their being conscious of the existence of these forces in them. And they lie so deep inside that they are unaware of their existence. Thus, many people, subject to these barriers, clamour about their dangers to others. For developing good decision-making ability, you have to develop the ability to carry out introspection from time to time, identify these barriers and start weeding them out. Sometimes, if you know there are blind spots, the decision may have to be postponed until the barrier is minimised. If you have identified your barriers but cannot get rid of them or minimise them, it would be advisable for you to seek professional help.

INDIVIDUAL VS GROUP DECISIONS

Groups are made up of individuals. However, there is evidence that groups sometimes help in arriving at more sound decisions than individuals can. Hence, the need for committees and boards in government departments as well as in private organisations. Two heads are better than one, but not always! There are occasions when groups can be ineffective. Groups can contribute a lot in making good decisions only if the majority of members are competent and share common goals.

But how do groups really function? Once individual views of the members are known, they start infecting others. Like biological susceptibility of humans, the virus of influence spreads, infecting the minds and thinking of other members. These members can either abandon their own view and align with the influential view; or else, rebel against the opposite view by working extra time to collect data to substantiate one's declared viewpoint. The majority generally aligns with the most influential personality rather than the opinion. This gives rise to sycophancy at work, or else individual prestige is at stake or revenge is at play.

But there are occasions when the expertise required for decision making may not be available. There may be an important aspect of the matter that may not have caught the attention of one individual. It is therefore desirable to seek expertise, feedback, ideas and opinions of others before finally deciding on long-term perspectives. Nevertheless, individuals in authority have corresponding responsibility for decision making, which they can shirk, only to their own peril, and their organisation's! You will receive both bouquets and brickbats. Don't grab only the bouquets and deflect the brickbats to committees and others; you will be caught red-handed.

Courses of Action

There are generally many options available before you to choose your course of action. But before making a choice, collect the facts about all available options. Evaluate each of these in the light of opinions of experts, your own experience, a parallel situation previously experienced elsewhere, and so on. Subject each option to logical and rational arguments; write down their advantages and disadvantages. Also analyse the requirements of time, space and resources required for implementation of each option. Lastly, in view of their *inter se* evaluation, which one do you find most advantageous?

Now reflect upon the following. Hard facts make one of the options/courses of action stand out over others. But how do you feel about its implementation? Does it suit your value system or is there a likelihood of some conflict arising? Would you like to smuggle goods to make more profit? Would you run a placement agency, beauty parlour, call centre with an innocuous name but dubious activities to make a higher profit? Your decision must be supported, both by your mind as well as heart.

You will not be content if your decision is mathematically based merely on facts. You will have to match your intellect with your feelings. Do this by reflecting over each course of action. Visualise the likely outcome of each course you adopt in the future. You will be surprised to find some of them acceptable, others not so; some exciting, some scary; some even repulsive.

Delve deep and ask more questions: 'What will it be like if I choose this course of action? What is the worst that could happen to me for this? Can I modify and make this course of action better? If this course of action is my best, how can I minimise its disadvantages? Which one of these will give me mental satisfaction, pride and cheer besides profits and advantages in material terms?' Remember, guard against taking impulsive decisions. Do not discard your intuition. When everything is analysed at length and you still feel uncertain to decide, follow the last resort — intuition or instinct.

Your Check-list for Decisiveness

The following check-list will be a quick reminder and guide to help you evolve and acquire effective decision-making habits:

- Remember, failing to take a decision is a decision to fail!
- Do not trespass into another's territory to make decisions that are not yours to make.
- Decision is a choice you are making from the alternatives available; not a prediction of right and wrong.
- Differentiate between impulsive decisions and speedy decisions. Move fast but don't rush.
- A right decision not taken in time is worse than a wrong decision taken in time.
- Do write down your decisions on paper to keep your ideas visible.
- Focus on what — not who — is right or wrong.
- Make notes of pros and cons of alternatives considered. It helps in making you think deeper and make better decisions.
- Don't create a backlog by postponing; it accumulates and becomes a burden. Continue making smaller decisions as you move on. A multiplying backlog will become a snowball to crush you under it.
- Involve people likely to be affected by your decision — to seek assistance, if and when required, or to take them into confidence. This way you enlist their commitment.
- The idea of obtaining cent per cent inputs or surety to

ensure the correctness of your decision is to apply a brake to your smooth running. No one can tell you the taste of the fruit of your decision, because fruition will be the result of action that is yet to take place in the future. So, take a risk and go ahead.

- Adopt the 'O-TARTS' approach:

(a) O - Objective must be unambiguously clear. Write it down.

(b) T - You must bind yourself in a specific time schedule in which to make a decision and implement the plan.

(c) A - All alternatives must be analysed and the most advantageous chosen.

(d) R - Resources required for implementation of the decision must be considered and mobilised.

(e) T - The decision being contemplated must foster team building.

(f) S - Positive and negative spin-offs of the decision must be considered to facilitate the positive spread and arrest the negative fall-outs, if any.

- The ideal decision is one taken by the majority at the lowest level and as close to the scene of action as possible. This is what it ideally should be. Pragmatism suggests that while you should be concerned about these aspirations of the people, you should go as low and as close as can be possible.
- Indecisiveness is an invitation to problems.
- Be proud and confident — you have the right to be wrong!
- Be bold and prepared to take on the consequences of your decision.
- Don't waste your time in being overwhelmed by trivialities. Think big; small things will fall in place as you move along.
- Foresee and devise effective risk-management and damage

control mechanisms by considering, 'What can go wrong with my choice of the option I am choosing,' or 'What measures need I take to prevent this likely loss/damage?' Don't be deterred; you can do it.

- Don't overwhelm yourself with everything. Delegate responsibilities for decisions to others too. Realign your limits.
- As part of your decision, also consider what administrative or technical changes may be required to facilitate its implementation.
- Think ahead and visualise what decisions might be required to be made before a simmering situation becomes a problem. Let ideas incubate in your mind; they will come handy when needed.
- Once you have made a decision, go ahead full throttle. Never curse yourself for the decision taken. It was right when you made it. The changed situation now may warrant modification or fresh decision. So focus on what is right now — and do it.
- Dream, contemplate and mentally rehearse implementation of your decisions.
- Make brain-storming a regular feature in your organisation. It will get you more ideas and commitment from your staff.
- Do not allow yourself to linger in the garb of collecting more inputs. Over-insurance is not payable.
- Brain-storming, discussions and deliberations must be focused on specific needs and have a time limit. Once a decision is made, discard all 'ifs and buts'. Put your shoulder to the grind and push without looking back.

Focus 5: Success Springs from Decision, Failure from Dithering!

- Be clear about your objectives and goals. Define and state them in writing, in brief.
- Decision making is a leadership function. Many kings and rulers were overthrown for indecision.
- Consider two types of strategies in life: short term and long term, with each short-term activity lending a push to the long-term activity.
- Dream and foresee requirements and opportunities opening up and prepare well beforehand.
- Discuss pros and cons of options with friends and experts to clear your mind of doubts, if any, and then decide.
- When faced with a dilemma, do not dither. Trust your intuition (not *jyotishis* astrologers!) and go ahead.
- As a leader, it is your authority to decide. As an authority, it is your right to be wrong too!
- Mistakes of commission are a lesser evil than mistakes of omission, for the dimension of the former is visible, but that of the latter remains hidden.
- Empower your decision making by co-opting modern technology, including IT and latest trends relevant to your trade/ profession. It will simplify your decision-making process.
- If you think you are in a deep dark hole and have no idea about what to do, decide to stop digging and look upwards — you'll see light!

SPECIFIC ACTION PLAN

A - Think of and briefly note down hereunder two major decisions — one right, one wrong — you made in your life in recent years.

1. ______

2. ______

B - When you think of the best decision made so far, did the risks taken by you fructify in your desired results? Enumerate the advantages you gained out of it.

______

C - Now, why did you make a wrong decision? What was not seen, not weighed, considered by you at that time? Enumerate reasons and losses suffered as a result:

1. Reasons for my wrong decision:

______

2. Losses suffered:

______

D - What are your dreams now? Dreaming must lead to thinking, thinking to planning and planning to action. If it is not happening to you, then you are again dithering. Decide on action today — and state it right here, now.

E - Review this page after a fortnight. Then revise and update it. And go ahead resolutely in pursuit of your dreams and continued success!

Kaalo ashvo vahati saptarashmih sahasraaksho ajaro bhuriretaah.
Tamaarohanti kavayo vipashchitastasya chakraa bhuvanaani vishvaa.

—Atharva Veda: 19.53.1

(The enormously mighty charger (horse) of Time, omniscient, extremely swift and dazzlingly bright like the Sun with seven colours of light, moves on forever along its orbit. The wise and prudent ride this charger of Time to success and power in this world).

6

Time Management

Ved Prakash's throat had been operated upon. He was convalescing in a cancer hospital in Delhi. There were no restrictions whatsoever on him; not even his smoking was barred — and he was a chain-smoker! He had all kinds of freedom and facilities in the ward. He could watch TV, read newspapers, magazines, talk to anyone on the phone, order whatever he wanted to eat and so on. The doctor visited him daily, enquired about his well-being and passed necessary instructions to the hospital staff.

Ved Prakash's jovial and friendly nature made him highly popular with everyone around. Everybody other than Ved knew about the terminal stage of cancer in his throat.

One day, finding him rather quiet and somewhat upset, the doctor enquired, "What's the matter Vedji, you aren't looking very cheerful today? Any problem?"

"Doctor I'm okay. But, each hour is like a day, and day like eternity. How to pass time is the biggest problem here?" Ved Prakash, unaware of the minuscule time left for him in this world, grumbled. His family members were informed by the doctor about the terminal stage and limited time left for him.

"How much time for him, doctor?" Ved Prakash's son enquired.

"It is difficult to say specifically. The deterioration will be now faster and it would be futile to spend more money on him because no substantial improvement is possible. We can only minimise his pain, suffering. He may live for six months or the end may come within days."

Ved was then informed of this. "What? Six months only? Oh no. Please, doctor, I'll give you whatever you ask for. Please give a few more years of life. I am only sixty and have no other problem. My father died at eighty; my mother lived a full 100 years. How can I die? Here, I give it up today; I swear I will never again smoke in my life. But please save me, doctor," said a frenetic Ved, throwing away his cigarette, and imploring as if seeking pardon at the gallows.

Ved stuck to his promise. He never really smoked again in life. He died two days later!

Time is a strange phenomenon in man's life. It is common to find people complaining, "*Pahar sa din… kaate nahin katata.*" (Day is an insurmountable mass….too difficult to scale). In the above case, Ved Prakash too felt harassed by this abundance of time but it was so only until he came face to face with the reality. When he knew the limited time available at his disposal, even six months did not appear enough where only a moment before, every minute, hour, day was too much of time! He frantically invoked even the heredity factor of longevity by citing the long years lived by his parents. He very much wanted to live up to eighty or 100 years. He was staking a claim to inherit those long years for a longer life and an ever-expanding future!

In another case, when Nagma and Aditya got married, they headed straight for Switzerland on a fortnight's honeymoon. They enjoyed visiting places, fun-parks, shopping arcades, restaurants and everything else. They had no time to ring up home; no time to attend to a couple of small assignments given to them by friends and parents.

"Sir, your flight is at 3 p.m. tomorrow. Do you want me to pick you up from the hotel or receive you at the airport?" the travel agent enquired on phone.

"Flight? Tomorrow? What flight are you talking about?" Aditya sought clarification, baffled and irritated.

"Your flight to New Delhi, of course! Tomorrow is June 28, Sir," the travel agent reminded him.

"Oh, no! Yes, I'm sorry.... Yes, okay, please pick us up from here..."

"Listen, Nagma! We came just the other day, *yaar!* He says it's over. We've to go tomorrow." whimpered Aditya.

"Oh no! And Aditya, we haven't had time for any shopping or talking to Papa's clients here..." Nagma too whined.

Nagma and Aditya spent a full holiday for a fortnight and felt as if they hadn't passed even a week. Time flew and they were unaware. They had all the time in the world and yet grumbled that they had no time! As a paradox, on the other hand, Ved Prakash has no time left for him and yet his grouse was that he had too much of time.

Something like this happens to all of us from time to time and we have different perceptions about time's pace. Curiously, time often seems to move at different paces under varying circumstances as you might have experienced so often in your day-to-day business.

Speed of time is inversely proportional to your speed; that is, if you move faster, time slows down for you. If you are lazy, inefficient and slow, time will run faster than you. For example, if X is running faster than Y, time will move slower for X but faster for Y. Or let us put it this way: Suppose X completes the race in forty minutes and Y in fifty minutes, X therefore has gained a lead of ten minutes. These ten minutes are available only to X, not to Y.

When you are involved in hobbies and interests, time flies, as it did for Nagma and Aditya. Researchers, writers, artists do not seem to have enough time. For active media reporters too, time seems to shrink and evaporate faster. This helps in saving energy. That's why they do not tire of doing or overdoing what they do.

Time slows down in darkness and boredom. This is what was happening to Ved Prakash. I will cite a personal example here that vividly explains this aspect. One day, I was busy in my study while Kamal, my wife, was watching her favourite TV programme. She had asked me to ring up and speak to our son, Varun who had just joined NDA at Khadakvasla (Pune). Since cadets do not have the privilege of having residential telephones in their cabins, I had arranged with the Academy authorities and Varun that I would call him up at 8.30 p.m. When I thought it was about time, I looked at the watch. It was 10.30 p.m., a full two hours past the time I thought it was. At first, I could not believe my watch, but then Kamal too confirmed that indeed it was 10.30 p.m. Varun had waited for my call and gone. Then suddenly the lights went off. Our inverter had already collapsed the previous day. In total darkness, Kamal and I spent enormous hours of the night, sitting in the balcony with mosquitoes feasting on us. After many long hours, finally the lights came on and we heaved a sigh of relief. Thinking it must be early morning hours, I looked at the watch; it was only 11 p.m. Those were the longest thirty minutes of that night for us.

Time seems to move very slow and very fast simultaneously in certain circumstances. For example, suppose you are going for an interview or a meeting, your cab develops a snag and the driver pulls to one side and starts examining the cab. You look at your watch every now and then, praying that he would move faster. In this state of mind, you notice that time to reach for the interview/meeting is running out. But at the same moment, you also feel that the cab driver is taking unduly long in repairing it. In case he mixes his humming and odd remarks on female pedestrians passing by — as is common with Delhi cab drivers —

it annoys you further, as you feel he is behaving so casual about it all. Both contradictory perceptions occur together in the same mind, at the same spot and situation!

Time has one more peculiarity — the same moment and period of time can appear different to different people, as someone has said: 'In youth, the days are short and the years are longer; in old age, the years are short and days longer.'

Francis Bacon has observed, 'A man who is young in years may be old in hours, if he has lost no time!'

What is 'Time'

There seems to be nothing in life that happens without reference to Time. Every action, endeavour and movement is time-bound. We hear expressions like: 'Bad times, good times'; 'Time will tell' and more. If one person says, 'Time heals all wounds,' another quips, 'Time wounds all heels!' What does one really mean when one uses both the expressions? What exactly is this phenomenon called Time? How do we define it? I tried to find out definitions. Great works of famous scientists like Einstein and Stephen Hawking overshoot common person's needs of daily life. Their explanations of origin of Time vis-à-vis the universe baffle us, even if we find them amusing and revealing. You feel like Alice lost in Wonderland. In our handling of routine life, we need a simpler meaning of Time just as we feel more comfortable calling water by its name and not by its symbols — H_2O. Your brilliance in chemistry notwithstanding, you still prefer to call a salt what it is and not sodium chloride. Try describing plants and flowers in your garden by their botanical names. Your listeners will switch off and walk away.

While scientists continue with their weird explorations, transcending mundane worldly affairs, we need to click with Time in easier and more direct manner. The different periods of Time like day and night, sunrise, sunset, mid-day, midnight, etc. are all constantly present on Earth; only locations change.

Divi Somo Adhi Shritah.

As is the Moon illuminated by the Sun, so are other planets (such as the Earth). So the day and the night are forever present.

The Central Idea

There is no moment ever when the time of your choosing (*shubha muhrat*) is unavailable for any good beginning. It is always the right time for you to start!

— Atharva Veda: 14.1.1

Are days, weeks, months or years Time? No, these are mere reference points or units of measurement by which we attempt to measure Time. But the early man perhaps had an easier journey through fewer reference points. Today one has to meander through multitudes of reference points and sub-points. Through the ages, man has played with Time. Time was when man was content with sunset and sunrise. Sunrise signalled him to start; sunset, to stop and relax. His body was his clock. His limbs told him when to relax, his belly told him when to eat and eyes when to sleep. But he was not content. As he advanced, his quest to speed up his life became intense. He began ruthlessly hacking his days into hours, hours into minutes, minutes into seconds and their proliferating progeny — micro-milli and nano-seconds... and so on. His Time-chopping exercise is yet not over!

So, instead of days, we now measure in hours, minutes, seconds and so on. But what is it that is being measured really? Is it some occurrence or change? Is it the span of our life or its parts? As per Nadine Gordimer, 'Time is change; we measure its passing by how much things alter' *(The Late Bourgeois World)*. But is that really so? Is it change that slows down and hastens or is it Time that contracts and expands in measuring the process and dimensions of change? A minuscule change like drifting of islands (e.g. Iceland from Europe) by a few metres occurs over hundreds of years. It would take thousands of years before the island covers a kilometre.

If the Darwinian Theory of Evolution is to be believed (everyone in the world seems to believe it), then man doesn't seem to have achieved much change considering millions or billions of years of evolution. We still retain vestiges and bear similarity to our forefathers in appearance and, sometimes, in behaviour too! Millions and billions of years roll by to see this little change. In sharp contrast to this, developments in the happening world are much faster. Nations are formed, destroyed and reformed in a matter of a couple of centuries. A life span of 100 years for humans goes through great experiences and transformations from childhood to old age. Such a life span is considered a great achievement — even envied, whereas, compared with evolutionary changes in Nature, a period of 100 years would appear like a milli-second. Are our days and years shorter than Nature's?

Austin Dobson says, 'Time goes, you say? Ah no! Alas, Time stays, we go!' *(The Paradox of Time)*.

Whatever our notions about Time, one fact is clear: life and evolution will have no meaning in the absence of Time. In fact, any existence without Time is unthinkable. It is impossible to perceive a happening without its relation to either past or present or future. Everything that touches consciousness spreads over Time. Conscious existence, in the absence of physical endeavour, too is an active happening. Therefore, if there is Time, there is existence and vice versa. There could be no creation if there were no Time. If so, isn't Time synonymous to life itself?

The direct relation of Time to our lives in today's material world has been succinctly yet lucidly explained by Benjamin Franklin when he said, "Remember that Time is money" *(Advice to a Young Tradesman)*. In *Poor Richard's Almanac,* his advice was even more pointed when he said, "Do you love life? Then do not squander Time, for that is the stuff life is made of."

John Randolph says, 'Time is at once the most valuable and the most perishable of all our possessions' (quoted by William Cabell Bruce in *John Randolph of Roanoke)*.

On consideration of different views of scholars and scientists, the following salient features of Time are seen:

- Realisation of existence is not possible without Time.
- Time is responsive to emotions.
- Time moves smoothly in happiness; sluggishly in sorrow.
- Time can neither be stored nor compensated.
- Time changes hues! (There are good times and bad times).
- Time is the most valuable but a perishable resource in life.
- We cannot control Time. (We can't manage it!).

Manage Yourself, not Time!

Kshanashah kanashchaiva vidyaamartham cha saadhayet.
Na tyaajyaou tu kṣhanakanaou nityam vidyaadhanaarthinaa.

(He who yearns for knowledge and prosperity must not abandon (waste) a *second of time* or even an iota of substance. He must invest each second to expand knowledge and wisdom, and each iota of substance to excel and prosper in life).

— Shukraneeti: 3/176

Impatient and worried looks, one hand pressing a mobile phone to the ear, the other shoulder wilting under the weight of a briefcase, a rolled up newspaper stuffed under the same armpit, unmindful of the world around, this haggard man is rushing to the lift daily at all hours in all government and business buildings. Who is he? It's you and it's us all! Why is it happening this way? Not enough time to do things, overburdened with work and responsibilities, nerve-breaking deadlines to meet, not getting even a weekend to spend time with family. "You see, I have been reduced to a mechanical robot," you bleat and whine in anguish. Can't we stretch Time a little more to suit our stretched up needs? Is there a different way to reorganise and restart? How to put an end to such nasty schedules so as to bring in some good times for ourselves?

Time is not in our control. Good or bad days and years will pass, irrespective of your desires or deeds. You cannot stop or store Time for later use. All the world's wealth cannot buy you an extra second. But you can organise yourself in a way that will entice good times and repel bad times. Good times will get over faster if you do nothing; bad ones will take longer time for inactive people. Conversely, if you launch yourself whole-heartedly in purposeful activities, good times will last and bad ones, disappear.

How can you manage your activities efficiently as to excel in your career and scale higher and higher in life through good times? Here are some guidelines that will help you somewhat in organising yourself.

There is no universally acclaimed time schedule that can fit in all spheres of activity and individual requirements. The type of schedule that you adopt would depend on your lifestyle, job, goals, priorities and other environmental requirements, if any. Nevertheless, if your new work schedule results in the following benefits, it would suggest that your choice of the schedule is working well for you:

- The change in your new work culture must meet your professional obligations efficiently.
- Your new-found relationship with Time should bring in new satisfaction and zeal.
- It must afford you time to enjoy your hobbies and interests too.
- It must help in fostering better relationships and happiness among those who love you.
- It must also ensure good care of your health.

Barbara Ehrenreich sums up the plight of today's upper middle-class society in her book, *The Worst Years of Our Lives* very aptly, this way, "I don't know when the cult of conspicuous busyness began, but it has become an important insignia of upper middle-class status. Nobody, these days, admits to having a hobby." It is indeed a sad, though unfortunately true, comment on our lifestyle.

There must be a way to live life to the full. Here are certain tested methods, which will help you in taking control of and managing yourself, or your time, which you can call *time management*.

START 'BUDGETING YOUR TIME'

Be it business, household or even personal expenses, everyone plans his finances to the minutest details. People seek expert advice from finance consultants on how to go about saving and investing their money. Housewives efficiently budget their household expenses, kitty shares, bills, etc., calculating to the last penny. You plan yours and, maybe, in your organisation a dedicated finance section does it for you. You are spending both — time and money — in your money-saving efforts. Ways can be found to create more money if you think you aren't making much now. For example, you may swap jobs, take up a part-time job in addition to your present job, take measures to enhance your sales through new strategies and so on. You can save and invest amounts of your choice. So, people can possess money in all variable quantities.

Time, however, is not money. Unlike money, Time is equitably distributed to everyone, though everyone has only twenty-four hours in a day, irrespective of their needs. It is not your earning; it is a gift, a present — or else why would your current Time be called present? For the enterprising, it is precious and limited; for the lazy it is a burden that has to be borne. It is they who talk of 'killing time'. For the suffering and dejected, it is apathy and misery unlimited! For the enterprising, more money can come through more efficient utilisation of Time. Time budgeting is an exercise whereby you plan and allocate segments of Time available for various activities over a period projecting into the future. This Time allocation must be reviewed from time to time. A comprehensive Time budgeting will cover all activities affecting your life — short term and long term. The short-term budgeting and planning has to be done daily and reviewed at least weekly. Long-term planning may spread from a year to a much distant future, depending upon your vision, dreams and goals.

To start with, you will have to withstand some discomforts in adhering to your budgeted plan of Time utilisation in your daily affairs. These discomforts are nothing but fallouts of a change syndrome. If you steadfastly adhere to the plan, inconvenience will disappear and you will soon adapt to the new, better and more efficient work culture. But if you abandon the effort after initial inconvenience, you will fall back to the same ditch from where you had planned to retrieve yourself. Therefore, reading this chapter or the complete book will not be of much use if you do not follow up your plans resolutely.

In institutional and governmental budgeting of finances, they have allocations for 'non-planned expenditure', 'contingency fund' and the like. In Time budgeting too, we must leave out 'cushion Time' to cater for interruptions, crises and any other unforeseen happenings that might require your indulgence — and, therefore, a chunk of your Time from other planned activities. If you have cushion Time, interruptions thus caused can be appropriately compensated.

PRIORITISE — 'FIRST THINGS FIRST'

The Black Cat Commandos (National Security Guard) in India are every VIP's blue-eyed boys. They are India's elite force.

Their role puts a heavy burden of responsibilities on them and every action by them has great significance.

Bhushan Bhatia, the Adjutant, used to take pride in doing everything meticulously. To achieve higher levels of efficiency, he had equipped himself with a computer, telephone, intercom, wireless sets and other gadgetry, neatly arranged on a long side-table. The table in front had heaps of files obscuring the table-lamp and Bhushan himself from public view.

To effectively pass orders, co-ordinate and follow up actions, he had four note-pads, one each for the group Commander, teams, office staff and local police. Besides, he maintained comprehensive 'To Do Lists' in his electronic diary as well as computer. Ved Marwah was the Director General, NSG, then. He had once observed that things were not very efficient in Bhushan's group. The group Commander also felt that, despite his sincerity and hard work, Bhushan (he would be busy in office almost round the clock!) was not producing results. No one knew why, until one day the reason emerged from his sincerity itself.

I had a meeting with the group Commander one day. As a result of our discussions, a number of instructions were to be conveyed to various departments. So, the group Commander spoke to Bhushan on the intercom and asked him to come. He gave out a number of points which Bhushan noted on his note-pad meticulously, acknowledging each point by a reassuring note of dedication: "Yes, Sir. Right, Sir. No problem, Sir..."

"That's all. Any questions?" the group Commander asked Bhushan.

"No, Sir. Everything will be done right away, Sir," Bhushan assured the boss.

"Okay then, get started," the group Commander concluded but, as Bhushan turned to leave the office, he told him, "Bhushan, please ask the head clerk to see me too."

Bushan turned, made a note on his note-pad and acknowledged again, "Right, Sir."

We had tea and a considerable time elapsed in discussions, but the head clerk did not appear. The group Commander pushed the button on the side of his desk and a smartly dressed commando appeared. "Sir?" he saluted and sought orders.

"Ask the head clerk to see me," the group Commander demanded softly.

The head clerk came, took the briefing from the group Commander and went away. Again, the group Commander pushed the button and instructed the commando to call the Adjutant. As Bhushan entered and smartly poised himself to take down fresh orders on his note-pad, the group Commander said, "Bhushan, please strike off the last point on your note-pad. I have taken action on it."

Bhushan, solemn and meticulous as ever, traced the last point relating to the head clerk on his note-pad and struck it. "Done, Sir," he confirmed in instant obedience. "Anything else, Sir?"

"No, thank you. You may go," the group Commander said brusquely.

Far from being meticulous, Bhushan's methods only added confusion. He created too many complexities even for simple things such that he found himself always at a loss. Bhushan was so involved in framing out his 'To Do Lists' on computer, electronic diary and assorted note-pads that there was no room for the right priorities to fit in. It was a case of missing priorities in one's efforts to prioritise! It was like Bhushan polishing firewood when more precious things in the house rotted and rusted.

You cannot do everything — small and big, urgent and routine, long term and short term — at one dot of Time. Even a lion sometimes fails to get a single prey from a herd of cattle in the jungle, despite chasing them. A hawk, on the other hand, happily glides high above in the sky, surveys the happenings on the ground, selects one prey and swoops straight onto it. Bhushan is a lion; not a hawk (incidentally, the appointment code for an Adjutant is also a lion!). He wants all in the herd to be his prey at one go! What happens? His greed starves in plenty.

In a disorganised environment, absence of priorities is the basic reason for all chaos. Draw out your priorities well as follows:

- Think a while and decide what is *urgent* and what is *important*.
- Keep your focus on the *important* but finish the most urgent one first.
- List out the rest of the requirements for the day in their order of importance.
- Be realistic in selecting only a few for the day, but ensure their completion.
- Update and review the progress daily.

- Things that cannot be done immediately but are important should have their schedule. Have a look at the goings on in your daily rounds.
- Have only three priorities (I, II and III), with your top priority having the least number of items.
- If you have two important things to do — one which you love to do, the other you dislike, do the latter first. This way both will be done faster and better.
- Let everyone know about your priorities.

Priorities navigate you properly and smoothly to your destination. You remain focused on the mission, with all resources appropriately mobilised. In the absence of priorities, you not only dissipate your time and resources but also run the risk of failing to achieve your target.

BE KNOWN FOR PUNCTUALITY

Merely reaching your office or place of work at the appointed time and signing the attendance register to avoid a tick-off or penal action is a very limited notion of punctuality. Punctuality, to be of value, must deliver. Value is added to it when a sense of punctuality is accompanied by commitment and loyalty.

Harish Garg, a software engineer and a team leader in a leading multinational software company was assigned a project that was very important for the company, considering the potential order it could attract from a number of insurance companies, within and outside India. The General Manager called and briefed Harish at length and gave him a deadline to give a presentation on the work carried out on the assignment, within a period of three months. Harish, a brilliant software engineer, found the project very easy and briefed his team hastily. He took it upon himself to finalise the project. He thought he could do it in a matter of five days flat! So, if it could be done any time, what was the necessity of doing it as an emergency? After the expiry of four months, Harish, thinking that he could do it any day, had to give an explanation for failing to submit an assignment; and, he lost the assignment as well.

The same assignment now came to Richa Aggarwal, a conscientious girl, though academically not as brilliant as Harish Garg. She accepted the assignment and agreed to submit the solution in two months time. She went running to Harish and told him about her assignment and sought help on friendly terms. She gave the presentation on the 30th day, i.e. a full month ahead of the deadline. The project was so well applauded that it was approved without any modification. Richa became a star of the company overnight.

What is being suggested here is:

- Never take simple things too simplistically.
- Bind yourself by guidelines. If these are not given, self-impose them more stringently.
- Have your own guidelines shorter than the ones laid down for completion of an assignment.
- Do not let your subordinates or team members know about the relaxations or liberties extended to you by the management. If so, you must have earned the liberties by establishing certain credibility about your efficiency and punctuality. Your bragging about such liberties will encourage your team members to exploit your popularity factor and go easy.
- Make this a rigid principle in life: 'Promise less, perform

more!' Study the assignment well at the beginning. Seek more time to accomplish it than you really think it will take. Ensure that you accomplish it much before the deadline, no matter what the odds.

- This method and style of working will surprise and delight your boss, clients and your very own team too.
- When you have nothing to do, ask: 'What's the best use of my time right now?'

You will create and reinforce everyone's faith in you more than ever before, besides saving time for your other projects or for an enjoyable weekend. Other spin-off benefits of this style will be:

- Development of a natural habit of learning more in a shorter time.
- Enhancement of your endurance capacity to give out higher value outputs, which will win you recognition, promotion and genuine popularity — and a bit of envy too.
- Acknowledgement of your credibility by all.
- Setting of a personal example by your efficiency, which will enhance your effectiveness as a leader.
- Availability of more time for your family and friends too.

Divide and Do!

There may be large responsibilities at home or in office for doing in a short span of time. For example, if you wish to construct a house, it will be a daunting task to accomplish in one go. The mammoth size of the project notwithstanding, you still must self-impose a deadline upon yourself for its timely completion. You will naturally plan in detail the site, size, architectural design, technical feasibility, financial aspects, time factor and so on. To take up the entire project at one time may be too cumbersome. But if you were to divide it into smaller segments and do it bit by bit, it will be done more easily and efficiently. You may, for instance, lay the foundation, and then, depending upon your financial planning, construct two rooms and the perimeter wall. Some of the large farmhouses and mansions have become the envy of neighbours as a result of this process.

The second part of this 'divide and do' theory is to relinquish the idea of being selfish or jealous. Help out others, whenever they need your help. As for your assignments, make full use of your team. Divide the assignment and share it as per expertise and experience of your team/staff. Teamwork is the backbone of any organisation. As a collective effort, it involves everyone on the mission at hand. This integrates the team more cohesively and gives each member a sense of belonging and importance. Besides saving time, it also economises on effort and enhances the quality of the output. This is how in a team you can go faster than time. Therefore, utilise the time left behind for value addition, supervision and refinement.

DELEGATE POWERS TO PROVE AND IMPROVE

You can't be doing everyone's work. If you are doing your subordinate's work just because he or she inefficient, you are neither helping the organisation nor the subordinate; nor even your own self. It is your responsibility to educate, train and improve your subordinates. Since they can't do it efficiently, so you do it; then you will continue piling up your own workload and they will continue piling up a serious liability on the organisation. Why are they there then? Try the following approach:

- Let everyone know that they are accountable for their

responsibilities, which may be charted or assigned by you.

- Be accessible to your subordinates for guidance and support, if and when required.
- Group the juniors and fresh entrants with experienced executives to learn and perform.
- Develop a system to monitor daily performance.
- Besides daily monitoring, have a fairly transparent periodical appraisal system.
- Listen to genuine problems and grant immediate redressal, wherever possible.
- Institute a regular training system in the organisation.
- Accept reasonable mistakes resulting from commission. Mistakes of omission should be viewed more seriously.
- Appreciate a good performance, applauding it in public.
- Now delegate. They will do it well with your guidance, if not on their own, to begin with.

As you know, people's working abilities do not always match their degrees. It is not uncommon to find engineers working as administrators and doctors managing hotels. In your team too, you will find people who have inclination towards particular activities. No one is totally useless. Only we fail to explore and tap the real talents of individuals. No one is evenly efficient in all fields. Somebody who is good in public relations may not be equally efficient in the assembly line. Somebody who is efficient in organising may not be so good in written work, accounts and so on. Even in learning, individuals exhibit their inclination and reluctance.

Get to know your people to the core. Dig out their efficiency and tap the real potential. If you delegate work to individuals in accordance with their competence, you will certainly get good results.

When you delegate, you give a chance to the subordinate to prove his/her worth and at the same time to improve his/her calibre. Hesitation in delegating proves that you do not have trust in your subordinates, nor do you have any interest in their professional improvement. You are working more and getting blamed too!

Your apprehension that you will have to do it yourself all over again because your subordinates are not capable of doing it is baseless, because there are a number of households and organisations, which are running very efficiently without you.

MONITOR PROGRESS

Every project needs time to be completed. To be worthwhile and fruitful, any work must have a plan, a time schedule and a monitoring mechanism. As the project progresses, it covers milestones on its way to completion. The journey becomes smoother if you check at various stages the mechanical fitness level of the vehicle, tyre pressure, oil levels, fuel consumption vis-à-vis distance covered and fresh requirements, if any. If deadlines for the completion are realistically worked out, keeping allowance for unforeseeable interruptions and slippages of time, the progress would generally match the plan. However, if you find the progress is slower than the plan, steps can be taken to speed up the progress.

It is through monitoring that you discover and evolve the tools needed for efficiency. Your interaction with the boss or client —

who also would be happy to be informed of the progress on the project from stage to stage — would often spring up new requirements or modifications in the project that is underway. Often it turns out to be a tedious and expensive job to incorporate desired changes once you have made progress to some extent. But sometimes such proposals come as a gift to you. The wonder drug penicillin was thought to be a useless contamination in a dish, but its usefulness was discovered in no time. Many historic innovations have come to us from serendipity, from chance discoveries.

INTEGRATE MODERN TECHNOLOGY IN WORK CULTURE

Rabri Devi was once visiting the lunatic asylum at Ranchi. Trying to look affable, she inquired of one of the inmates, "Have you any idea of the time?"

The inmate grinned. "Certainly, Madam ji," he replied, "Just one moment, please." He whipped out a long ruler from his pocket and held it in the sunlight. Then he marked out the shadow that was made, and did some rapid calculations. He fiddled with a compass and a plumbline, and then turned to the hon'ble Chief Minister. "Madamji," he declared triumphantly, "it is exactly sixteen minutes past eleven o'clock."

"Wow, that's marvellous!" cried Rabri, thoroughly amused. "But tell me how did you really do it?"

"Oh, it's just one of those things that can be learnt. I have studied it. I tell by the sun," the inmate claimed modestly.

"Excellent!" said Rabri. "But tell me what do you do when it rains or it is night time?"

"Oh," he shrugged, "I have got something for that, too."

"What's that?" urged the Chief Minister, appreciating the talent and evincing new interest.

The inmate smiled. "Well," he answered proudly, "in that case, I simply look at my watch!"

This 'talented' inmate was not only rewarded with cash awards and honour, but there was serious lobbying for him to be appointed as Director of Education in the state. As pressure is mounting on the Chief Minister, she is said to be favourably disposed to the idea.

Sticking to outdated modes when simpler and more efficient systems are available to function more efficiently is sheer madness. There are employees in offices who use outmoded modes of working. The faster they change, the better it would be.

Due to technological advancement, we are witnessing new wonders unfold every day. Never before in the recorded history of mankind has so much been achieved over centuries and millennia as in the last 100 years. Advances made in telecommunication and computer sciences have put virtually everything in a plate before us. Ready-made solutions are available for assorted applications. There are tools and technologies that help us in adapting, modifying or innovating, be it in designing, manufacturing, accounting, marketing, advertising, learning or educating — we have it all on our desk, just a click away.

However, despite these strides in technology, there are still people who are reluctant to break away from the old methods and outdated work culture. They do not wish to change because they have got used to what they have inherited from their predecessors. They do not want change; they stick to old habits, well aware that progress means change. It is never too old to learn and lead — or at least be at par with others. Explore and invest in new ideas and technology. It will put you in the lead.

In some offices, I find computers and assorted high-tech gadgetry arranged in an impressive array but with no one using them. Installing high-tech equipment is one thing; to put it to efficient use is another. What is the point in installing a gadget, which no one knows how to operate? Training also must be given equal importance to develop talents to match the new equipment. In their absence, installation of new machines will be a wastage of time, money and effort. To be of value, machines and human effort must be appropriately integrated.

Leading industries have this philosophy of integrating modern technologies and new ideas in-built in their organisational structure. Their Research and Development (R&D) wings are ever on the prowl for innovating, adapting and moving ahead with the latest in technology. Someone has said, "If you were to pray for only one thing, let it be for an idea." If you are doing it all very well until now, think of how you can do it better in the future. That is the ignition key for your progress. You will be pleasantly and profitably surprised — progressive change proliferates profits and Time.

Hobbies and Entertainment

All work and no play make Jack a dull boy. The harder the people work, the more they require to recoup and recharge. We must have a holistic view of our life, career or business. Our time plan, therefore, must encompass the entire life. Job, family, friends, health and entertainment are all essential parts of life. Judicious allocation of time for all these activities help us lead a balanced life. We are then more appropriately poised to take on any problem.

On getting tired of the day's heavy and onerous commitments, many people take recourse to alcohol for mental relaxation. The hangover next morning either holds them back from attending the day's business or even if they do make it to the office, they are unable to concentrate on their work.

If you wish to seek relaxation — mental and physical — shift from alcoholic addiction to healthier hobbies. An hour in a gym will take good care of your health and make you feel more energetic throughout the day. A regular yoga regimen will make you feel rejuvenated and younger too! Your output will be decidedly better, both qualitatively and quantitatively. Try it for a fortnight and write to me if you fail to achieve what I have promised here you will.

Besides a regular health care programme (yoga, aerobics, gym or jogging), do take time off periodically to go out — far away to a place where Nature abounds. It could be a picnic or a holiday trip to some scenic place or both. These periodic breaks from your routine working environment allow you to look at your work from different angles while you holiday in real leisure. This is exactly what Prime Minister Atal Bihari Vajpayee does when he composes poetry or pens down his *Musings* while on a holiday in Manali. When you return from such outings, you do feel recharged and your performance and relations improve.

DEVELOP THE COURAGE TO SAY 'NO'

Some people in government offices and public sector units do have the courage, nay arrogance, to say 'no'. There are people who place their briefcase on the desk and disappear for a good part of the day on undisclosed missions. When given some assignment, they whine: "But, it is none of my job"; "It's already 5 o'clock"; "Why can't you find someone else to do it?" This is not the kind of 'no' that I am suggesting. This is a product of negative attitude and has a narrow aim — shirk responsibility.

The idea behind my advice is a healthier one for both — the individual and the organisation. Loyalty to your organisation should guide you when to say 'no'. If you cannot do a job within the stipulated time, you must either have the deadline extended or divide the work to share as a team. If you accept the responsibility and fail to accomplish, it tarnishes your image and may cost the organisation dearly too. Assignments and responsibilities accepted reluctantly will put you under heavy stress, consume all your time and yet will not be accomplished in the manner and standard expected. Nobody therefore gains in situations like these. If you have genuine concern for your organisation, you will understand the importance of the job, and when you say 'no', it would be with the intention to offer better options. Hard work does not kill, hard feelings do. So, do not punish yourself by accepting what you will not enjoy doing.

Fix Your Peak Efficiency Hours

Human performance is governed by peculiarities of individual biorhythms. There are people, though a very small number, whose performance is not significantly altered from morning to evening. There may be some who work more efficiently in the evenings. But most people enjoy working in the morning hours and produce better output than they do in the afternoons. Judge for yourself and find out your peak efficiency hours. Then organise these few hours to do those jobs that demand higher concentration and labour. For instance, if morning hours are your peak efficiency hours, you will benefit more, if you were to reach your workplace a little earlier than routine office time. This extra hour can be adjusted subsequently elsewhere. This will allow you peaceful, uninterrupted time to produce high quality work.

When you have a heavier or a more difficult job at hand, it would require more concentration, energy and time — all of which you can best afford only in your peak hours. Postponing difficult work tires you more and ends up in procrastination. The early morning freshness in the environment and your unspent energy can be best utilised in doing such jobs more efficiently.

The jobs that you enjoy doing because they are either simple or interest you in some way, should be fixed for, say afternoons, when most people feel dull after lunch. A job of your interest will take away your dullness and get done well too.

'Audit' Your Time Spending

On a summer morning, Emperor Shahjahan once rode far away from the Red Fort. By noon, he strayed into a field. The farmer was honoured to have His Majesty in his fields. He extended courtesies with a lavish heart, offering specimens of whatever produce he had in the field. Reciprocating the gesture, the Emperor presented a pearl necklace to the farmer and asked, "You look very sturdy and healthy. What's your age?"

"I'm sure I have been through sixty or seventy summers," the farmer said gleefully.

"You mean to say you have not kept count of the years you have lived?" the bemused Emperor queried.

"Your Majesty, I always count my oxen, buffalo, my farm produce, my *pagri*, my *hookah* and every property I have. But as for my years, I know nobody who wants to steal them, and I shall surely never lose them," the Jat dumbfounded the Emperor with his irrefutable logic, even if utterly crude and rustic. The Emperor returned to the Red Fort with the Jat philosophy ringing in his ears.

Agreed, no one else is going to steal your years, but if you are not careful about them, you may squander them with much worse results. If you can't keep count of your time, you cannot keep control of your life either. A periodic review of your activities vis-à-vis time will be of great value. Develop the habit of taking stock of your daily activities in the evening and reasoning out why a particular action in your 'To Do List' could not be completed. Do you think you spent your day the way you had planned? Would you like to spend your tomorrow any differently? A stocktaking or an audit of hours spent during the day will be a revealing exercise, which will yield a number of lessons to be learnt.

Likewise, a weekly time-audit exercise is very desirable. This exercise should not be confined to individuals; it should cover the group to find out how each spent his/her time. What was possible in X hours and what was achieved? Find out where things did not progress as per the planned schedule; identify the major time-wasters and take corrective measures. Do take note, though, that time spent in planned entertainment and rest is not a waste.

Do not, however, embark upon economising on time and money like the old woman who, when she called a watch repairer to repair her electric clock, received the reply, "There's nothing wrong with the clock. You didn't have it plugged in," the repairer observed.

"I don't want to waste electricity, so I plug it in only when I want to know what time it is!" the woman replied.

Gatey shoko na kartavyo bhavishyam naiva chintayet.
Varttamaanen kaalen pravartante vichakshanah.

(Wise people do not repent for what has gone past nor do they worry about the problems of the future. They fall in tune with the present and do their best).

— Chanakya Neeti Darpanah: 13/2

GOOD TIMES LIE AHEAD!

Don't worry if you have wasted time in the past. Worrying will waste it even more. Now detach yourself from the past and move forward. If you had wasted money, you would have been poorer. But as for time, you still have all the time in the world. You are assured of a daily gift of twenty-four hours — no matter what you do with it.

If you kill time, the danger is that you would be buried under the debris of the future. There is a pertinent warning-cum-advice which I reproduce here. I had taken it down in my diary some time ago. I regret my inability to mention its author's name, which I missed out at that time.

Time Budgeting and Audit Sheet

I. Time Budget

No.	*Normal/Healthy Requirements*	*Time (Rqd.) (hrs.)*	*Total (hrs.)*	*Remarks*
1.	Sleep	7	7	
2.	Personal hygiene and early morning chores	1	8	
3.	Physical health care (yoga, gym, aerobics, walk/jog, etc.)	1	9	
4.	Spiritual care: meditation, introspection, mirror exercises, etc.	30 mins.	9 hrs. 30 mins.	
5.	*Newspapers, magazines*	40 mins.	10 hrs. 10 min.	
6.	*TV, telephone and Internet surfing*	1	11 hrs. 10 min.	Housewives and retired people can afford more time here.
7.	*Self-education, writing practice*	1 hr. 30 min.	12 hrs. 40 min.	
8.	*Rest (daytime siesta)*	1	13 hrs. 40 min.	Optional.
9.	*Social courtesies*	1	14 hrs.	Not a fixed daily requirement.
10.	*Sports, games/hobbies*	1	15 hrs. 40 min.	
11.	*Office/business*	8	23 hrs. 40 min.	

"The ticking of the clock is one of the most important things in the world, for it marks the passage of time. It reminds us that another second, another hour, another day has gone. And yet, despite this constant reminder, most of us go along using time aimlessly, failing to get out of it either by enjoyment of life or satisfaction of accomplishment. We know that the opportunity that today presents will never be repeated; that spring fades into summer, and soon winter comes, and we wake with a start to realise that another year has passed. Still we postpone. 'There is plenty of time', we tell ourselves. That is the great fallacy. *The clock of life is wound but once!*"

Note 1 : Turning life into a clockwork robotic machine will be the antithesis of what is being advocated here. This is to be used as a check-list so that in the daily humdrum of chaotic lifestyle in towns, you do not overlook things that may look small but are bricks for the foundation of your life.

Note 2 : The italicised areas are expected to be flexible due to certain fluctuations in your daily requirements. So, make changes as and when required. If you have observed, only a small fraction of four hours only (serial 2, 3 4 and 7) is recommended to be followed with resolute determination. Do it regularly for at least forty days. You will enjoy the change immensely.

2. Time Audit

Time Waster	*Possible Causes*	*Suggested Remedies*
Unplanned functioning	• Ambiguity in direction/policy. • Unclear targets. • Poor vision of future. • Poor knowledge of environment.	• Devise clear directions/policies. • Assign clear-cut targets. • Remember, the time you invest in planning is never wasted. In the end you save more time. • Make it time-bound; mark various stages to monitor progress.
Inverted priorities	• Ignorance of goals and objectives.	• Set and declare clear goals and objectives.

(Contd.)

	• Lack of motivation. • Confusion on policies.	• Involve people in planning. • Set and disseminate clear policies.
Excessive/ unncessary paperwork	• Seen as an indicator of knowledge; show off. • Lack of faith: put it on record as evidence of your doing; not ensuring to do!	• Encourage direct interaction and decisions on handwritten notes. • Encourage sharing of information on computer network. • Encourage highlighting of brief, minutes and speed-reading.
Routine and trivial	• Casual work-culture. • Lack of motivation.	• Enforce healthy work culture and discipline.
	• Over-supervision. • Sense of fear/insecurity.	• Focus on results, not methods. • Encourage innovation and creative ideas.
Visitors	• Permissive/non-professional office-culture. • Non-availability of requisite information at Reception. • Non-adherence to visiting hours. • Casual attitude and misplaced courtesies.	• Display and publicise visiting hours at Reception. • Integrate front office in computer network to make available information usually in demand. • Maintain record; ask purpose of visit.
Telephone calls	• Lack of training in telephone etiquette. • Casual office atmosphere. • No call-screening system.	• Institute call-screening system. • Educate your secretary to handle calls rather than plugging you to every call. • Let the answering machine do it for you even when you are there. People cannot gossip with machines — queries will be precise.
Meetings	• Confused agenda. • Inability to decide individually. • Need for advice/suggestions. • Unclear ideas; straying from main issues/agenda items.	• Try giving serious thought to the issue; you will have the answer. • Discuss with one or two experts only. • Decide not to have meetings unless major issues or policies

(Contd.)

		are required to be discussed.
Over-centralisation	• Lack of faith in system. • Feeling of insecurity. • Faulty organisational infrastructure. • Fear of loss. • Keenness for over-insurance.	• Decentralise and delegate decision making. • Do not meddle in others' domain; they'll come, if need be. • Give quick and bold decisions. • Take risks. • Accept mistakes of *commission;* discourage *omission*.

Note:

1. Review and audit your last week's Time utilisation in the light of your own objectives.
2. How do you feel now? Had you allocated enough time to achieve those objectives? If they were not achieved, what was the reason?
3. Check on the time-wasters and take measures now. Mark those time-wasters who take a toll on your time and be ruthless in eradicating the causes of it.

Focus 6: Time is Your Life; Don't Squander It!

- Time is the most precious resource. While other resources may vary, this you have as much as the most successful person in the world.
- Time is also a continuously depleting resource. You cannot store it; you can either use it or lose it.
- Inculcate a do-it-now habit. Do not procrastinate.
- Every morning begins with a fresh gift of twenty-four hours of opportunities for you. Welcome these with positive thought and action.
- Imbibe self-discipline and respect for time — budget it and audit your spending.
- Divide and do. Don't carry everybody's load on yourself. *Right person for right job* will speed up your accomplishment.
- Delegate and decentralise decision making. Don't keep people waiting for your decisions or looking over the shoulder for every turn on the road.

(Contd.)

- Monitor progress by going where the work is; not by calling people to your office.
- Periodically review and modify plans, if required.
- Do plan time for hobbies, entertainment and holiday trips with family to recoup and recover.

SPECIFIC ACTION PLAN

A - Think of the best opportunity you have ever lost in life. Now at least you can think of reasons for that loss. Write them down here.

____

____

____

____

____

B - How are you seeking and exploring for fresh opportunities — interacting with achievers, reading and studying current and futuristic trends? Think and write down your methods of such exploration.

____

____

____

____

____

C - What are your 'peak efficiency hours'? Plan doing your most difficult and important work in these hours. Budget these hours accordingly. Specify your immediate, toughest and important work here and now.

____

____

D - Carry out an analysis of your preceding week's performance. Are you satisfied with the time invested and the results achieved? If not, how do you plan your next week to ensure better results? Write down your observations and intentions/outline plan.

"Yajjaagrito duuramudaiti daivam tadu suptasya tathaivaiti.

Duurangam jyotishaam jyotirekam tanmei manah shivasankalpamastu."

—Yajur Veda: 34/1.

(Oh Lord! the mighty spirit (Manah) that is capable of reaching the farthest corner of imagination and achieving the toughest of goals, resides in me. It has boundless vigour to initiate and influence action in consciousness. Active and penetrative even in my unconscious state, it is also capable of unleashing infinite potential in ruling and focussing my senses and desires. Let that innate power drive me with utmost determination to my pious, noble Goal.)

7

Goal Setting and Life Planning

Why does everyone talk about goals? Why has the word 'goal' become so significant in life? The answer is simple: without goals, you cannot reach anywhere. Among reasons for failures and frustrations afflicting modern society, absence of specific goals is a major one. The casual and short-sighted approach to life lies exposed when you come across people caring more for their cars than for their spouses. There are many who pay heavily for their own health care and yet flout the doctor's instructions and drink, smoke and do all that is forbidden for their own good.

You find people making resolutions on the eve of New Year and breaking them by the end of January — some break their promises the very next morning. The more they break their own resolutions, the more frustrated they feel — desperately trying to escape from an invisible enemy! They feel the world is designed for their entertainment and it owes them care and pleasure.

The *Declaration of Independence* is a historical and constitutional document of the United States of America. It guarantees citizens of the US, *'life, liberty, and the pursuit of happiness'*. Benjamin Franklin, who was instrumental in drafting the document, aptly pointed out later, "All our nation guarantees is the pursuit of happiness. You have to catch up with it yourself!" But people still feel the government owes them happiness.

Health, well-being, pleasure and happiness are all very desirable things in life. But can any amount of money buy any one of these for us from a shop? If happiness, into which every other achievement seems to merge, were the objective of life, it would still be intangible and highly volatile in nature; it is not distinctly visible. You cannot catch something that is not tangible, not definite. To achieve happiness you have to first visualise it; and if you are able to see it, you can surely draw up your road-map to it. That is what the whole idea of goal setting is all about.

Chanakya explains it succinctly and warns us against abandoning goals halfway in the following couplet:

Yo dhruvaani parityajya adhruvam parishevate
Dhruvaani tasya nashyanti adhruvam nashtameva cha.

(He who abandons pursuit of specific substantial goals and runs after illusory fantasies ruins what could be truly his. His illusory fantasies — tantalising mirages, were in any case not there. Straying from the pursuit of specific goals to pursuit of a mirage is thus self-destructive).

— Chanakya Neeti Darpanah: 1/13

Why do people abandon their pursuits halfway? In my interaction with people from assorted backgrounds, I have found the following main reasons for it:

- Vague and hazy goals.
- Inadequate knowledge and preparation.
- Impatience.
- Lack of self-confidence.
- Poor feedback and monitoring mechanism.
- Exaggerated view of routine/foreseeable problems.

Manish Walia was a software engineer in a multinational company in Bangalore. Krishna Muthappa, his class-fellow and a close friend, launched his ad paper for local circulation in the same city. Initially planned to be a fortnightly, the paper did well and Krishna was soon flooded with ads. He converted it into a weekly and began doing good business within six months of its launch. Manish Walia, who used to frequent Krishna's home and office, watched the progress of Krishna's business with awe and envy! Manish would often return to his room brooding. He thought he was wasting his time in the company where he was not earning even one-third of what Krishna was earning.

Manish decided to quit his job and launch a similar ad paper in Gurgaon, his hometown. Within a month of his return to Gurgaon, he launched the paper as a weekly publication. In three months, he went broke; he could not clear the printer's bills and had to abandon the venture.

Friends, relatives and well-wishers came, sympathised and gave mixed comments, opinions and advice — sought and unsought! Manish liked Anil Mehta's views and started spending most of his time in the latter's company. Mehta offered Manish partnership of a transport company he was planning to start. They pooled in their resources, raised loans with joint liability and purchased four trucks.

Unfortunately, however, they could not celebrate their first anniversary. They had to sell the property at scrap rate. Mehta did retain one truck for himself and continued his solo efforts with modified plans. Manish felt finished and resigned himself to the cruel Fate, spending most of his time brooding and associating with those who had either likewise failed or had always been non-starters.

Gradually he grew more impatient and angry at every failure. "It's foolish to invest your own money in today's world. Why don't you start something where you need not invest anything other than your time and where returns in terms of money and *izzat* (honour) come in tons?" a friend suggested.
"What's that?" a salivating Manish asked.

"Come with me. I'll introduce you to the PS to Dukhram, the minister...,"

Manish bit the bait thrown in by the friend. His proximity with the power-pillars in politics soon armed Manish with influence and arrogance.

Manish made collections from ambitious entrepreneurs in search of patronage and favours. Victims of his extortions also included a number of innocent, unsuspecting rich aspiring to be in the good books of the minister. He soon graduated to kidnapping and murder for money. He bought a beautiful farmhouse on the Gurgaon-Jaipur highway where his dreams to live and enjoy a contented and happy life lay buried; he lay on the death-bed. Manish has been running for his life for the past two years even as the police and the revengeful victims are hounding him.

Today, his wife, suffering from cancer of the uterus, languishes haplessly on her death-bed at the farmhouse, with a three-year old daughter and ailing parents-in-law watching life go past. Friends, relatives or well-wishers — no one comes to see them any more. The farmhouse that once glittered with life now looks dreary and haunted, with the eerie silence broken by none other than the police — the only callers!

Arthamidvaa u arthina aa jaayaa yuvate patim.
Tunjaate vrishnyam payah paridaaya rasam duhe
vittam mei asya rodasee.

(As people with laudable goals achieve healthy relationships and usher in marital bliss and happiness in their family lives, and as does the infinite energy from the Sun and lightning nourish and empower the Earth and its resources, showering prosperity all over, so must you prepare and arm yourself with knowledge and inspiration from those who are learned in appropriate sciences to achieve your goals to eliminate sorrow and misery from life).

— Rig Veda: 1.105.2

Manish had everything: education, professional qualification and experience in computer software, an encouraging and caring family background, and opportunities for the asking! But he ruined not only his life but also that of his family. Why? Because he had everything except the goal! What he thought were his goals were mere wishes, craze and lust which drove him mad.

He was sure to crash; and which he did.

Dream, Desire and Plan

If you are clear on the significance of goals in life, then let's do a small exercise. We have already discussed enough about time in the previous chapter. While doing the 'Specific Action Plan' there, you must have nurtured some new ideas, even though hazy and fluid. What are your dreams? How do you visualise your future life? Take time off other activities now for an hour. Select a quiet place where no one can disturb you, and reflect over what you have been thinking, cherishing and desiring in life. Don't keep on hopping from one desire to another. Evaluate in your own way and decide which is your most important desire in life. It is most likely that your desire would be to achieve a definite objective — which objective is a different issue! Now concentrate on your ideas as follows:

- Identify the objective to see it vividly.
- What stages do you visualise to cover on your way to your objective?
- How do you plan to reach the first stage?
- Have faith in your ability to carry out that plan.
- Start and don't be disheartened by errors — trial and error too is a method.
- Periodically review your work to reach the goal without losing sight of your immediate and final objectives.

Paul C. Fisher, often quoted in management schools and industry, was literally on the road after his Fisher Armour Manufacturing Company lost and crumbled in the 1950s. He took personal loans to restart, but sank still deeper in debt. One day he took time off to contemplate. He had dealt with tools and machinery for years. He knew that it was easy to fool people but impossible to fool machines. If a machine is to run efficiently, it must be tuned and set up properly. It occurred to him that the same scientific technique would be required in running the business. He went through the introspective exercise described above and drafted a set of rules to govern his personal actions and another set of rules, written objectives and policies to govern his business actions. The result was remarkable. Paul Fisher was soon on top of the business again after repaying back his debts.

Goal setting has been variously described by different people, primarily to highlight the specific needs of their organisation or people. Management by objectives, management for results, goal seeking, planning and so on — all point to one destination: achievement of results.

Most people hate to plan; they think it a waste of time. Yes, it will be a waste of time if not followed by action. But action initiated on slip-shod plans will be a gross wastage in terms of time, effort and resources too. Experienced managers and military Commanders say, '*Time spent in planning is never wasted.*' A civil engineer friend of mine is working in a company that was responsible for construction of two important flyovers in Delhi. Resisting the pressures to hurry up in one of the meetings, he said "Cutting short planning may save us a few days and a few lakhs in monetary terms, but an extra hour at drawing and redrawing the plan on board may save many precious lives in the future and perhaps even cost in long-term analysis — for our reputation matures up with it."

Why do people shy away from planning? Because of impatience

in today's environment of quick-fix solutions. A doctor who refers patients to lab tests to confirm his/her diagnosis is not as popular as the one who administers heavy antibiotic doses and which show the results within hours. Everyone knows it is important for healthy living to have a disciplined regimen with regular physical exercise and abstinence from over-drinking or over-eating. But that is only important; not urgent. Impatience has taught us to do only urgent things because we can no longer push them any further. Living crisis-to-crisis has become the dirty norm. Although it is important for us to go the gym regularly, but we don't. When it becomes unavoidably urgent for us to go to the doctor because we can't bear the pain, we rush to him.

Planning too, though important, is never urgent. We find ourselves so heavily surrounded by the routines of daily life and intermittent emergencies that we easily put off planning to another day, another week. If we were think to a little harder, we would find it better to devote our attention and time to planning, then the emergencies and urgencies that surround us now would automatically disappear soon. It is like the operations conducted by the security forces to prevent terrorists from striking their targets. There is no knowing how many terrorist attacks have been foiled and how many lives have been saved. In an incident where terrorists strike and leave behind five dead bodies does become a ghastly scene in contrast to saving of hundreds of lives that could have been likewise claimed by terrorism. The moving spirit in such perceptions is not logical; it is psychological.

Another reason why people fail to think deeply and plan well is that they are in a hurry to get rid of their workload — the sooner the better. Think of your days when you were just a fortnight or so away from your finals. Even though you were not fully satisfied with your preparations, you still wanted the exams to be over soon. There are managers who are rushing through even before the job has been adequately described. Impatience makes them jump to the results; and when results do not come up to their expectations, they feel frustrated.

Often, planning becomes difficult because of vague and unclear goals. When goals are not specifically stated in measurable terms, plans run adrift. It is in such situations that people plan to cover imponderables and be cent per cent sure in planning even when they are not so sure about the shape of their goals. Sometimes goals are not clear because they are not our goals. Manish Walia's plans went awry because he was copying others for very superficial reasons. He was going by whims and quirks; not by goals based on solid reasons. When a goal is anchored to your ambition, and a strong desire to accomplish it — be it in a profession, family life or any aspect of life, it propels you further. What is needed is a strong desire to accomplish, which alone will ignite your potential and boost your commitment.

We come across friends and relatives who would not give up their bad habits, like smoking and drinking. A good majority of them seem so powerless when they say, "I tried my best but I have a very weak will power...can't give it up." These 'weak will-power' people also include those who are controlling business empires, armies and great institutions. But when the doctor explains the danger to their health, they change their habits in a day. Why? Because they now have a *good reason* that also gives them the *commitment* to do it. So, it is not the *'weak will power'*; it is the reason and commitment that makes it happen.

CONCRETISE YOUR PLAN!

Be it your personal life, your business or your career, goal setting does make a difference between mediocrity and excellence. Your desires and ambition incubate it; your plan provides it the wings and your commitment makes it fly high. To enable efficient hatching and goal fetching, here is the nest where you do it all:

- **Burning yearning:** You must kindle a strong yearning to achieve the goal. Your ardent desire is the ignition key to start you. Do not leave it lying latent in an obscure corner of your heart. It will starve and die if not cared, fondled and stroked from time to time.
- **Statement of your goal:** Let your desires crystallise. Identify and write down your goal and display it in bold writing on the wall over your table, where you spend most of your time, to enable you to see it often. Make it a point that your goal is specific, time-bound and unambiguous. It must be challenging and yet realistic. When you do so, it does not remain on paper alone; it gets etched on your subconscious. Look at the following examples:

Unclear Goals	*Clear and Measurable Goals*
• To become a doctor.	I shall qualify for entry into AFMC, Pune by June 2003.
• To increase profit.	I shall enhance sale by 20 per cent in north India by 30 November 2003.
• To reduce wastage.	We shall reduce scrap level to 3 percent by 31 October 2003.
• To improve living standard.	I shall purchase a three-bedroom flat in Chandigarh by April 2004.

- **Time analysis:** Evaluate your current level in relation to the goal and calculate realistically how much time you need to accomplish your goal. Then set it as your deadline.
- **Influencing factors:** Now consider all the factors that are likely to influence your plan in either way — some may become obstacles in your path while others would assist you in reaching your goal, viz:
  - ***Self-preparation:*** You might need to acquire more knowledge through training, study, liaison visits, discussions and so on. Integrate this preparation into your planning.
  - ***Finance:*** You will perhaps need money. Compute your requirements realistically and comprehensively. How will you build up these funds? Consider loans from friends, relatives, banks and other financing institutions in the light of their terms and conditions. You may not need all the funds immediately. Your final plan will suggest when and how much you need at various stages. Initiate action to procure these funds accordingly.
  - ***Space:*** It is the nest where you plan to hatch your goal. The nature of your goal will determine the location and infrastructure needed to start with. It may be an intermediate arrangement to economise initially — even a corner of your living premises — but it must assist you in moving forward.
  - ***People:*** You might need some technical hands, skilled or unskilled labour, depending upon the nature of your goal. You will have to hunt for the right kind of people.
  - ***Market:*** Whatever you do, you need a clientele to buy what you will sell. Market is not only to sell goods. Even

if your goal is to preach as *pujari* (priest), or work as a social worker or contest elections as a politician, you do need a market for your services — be it of devotees, area or vote bank. Can you sell anything unless you have buyers? Target your market and devise your strategies to cultivate it: liaison, contacts, advertisements, presentations and so on.

- ***Obstacles:*** It is essential to visualise the obstacles and problems you are likely to encounter in your pursuit. If you have pragmatically analysed and tentatively planned how to counter and surmount these obstacles, you will find the going easier. Remember, there is no problem on earth that does not have a solution. Those who are on top today are only those who took the challenge and surmounted the odds; those who turned away from the odds are at the bottom and will remain so until they get up and move ahead.

- **Execution:** Having analysed all the factors mentioned above, you are now in a position to plan specific actions. Decide and write down your priorities and activities — each with a time frame. Assign specifics to yourself and others: tasks, time, resources and terms of reference, if any. Fill up all the gaps in *what, where, how* and *how much,* by *whom,* by *when.* Prepare a time-table to execute your work plan. Since every moment is a precious moment for the initiation of a good pursuit, decide now and proceed.
- **Perseverance:** Once begun, there will be occasions that would be cheering. Sometimes it would seem you were better off than landing yourself in trouble by choosing this endeavour. These are feelings which every marathon race-winner goes through when he or she has done all but the

last mile. He or she feels exhausted; wholly finished. But on completing it, all the lost energy returns and swells, for it brings additional benefits too: satisfaction, pride, recognition, honour and more. Therefore, let no setback sap your energy or dilute your resolve. Remain positive and determined. If need be, review or modify your plan in the light of new inputs. But give up — NEVER!

Yaddooram yadduraaraadhyam yachcha doorey vyavasthitam,
Tatsarvam tapasaa saadhyam tapo hi duratikramam.

(If what you desire is too far, that which is too fascinating and yet beyond reach even for adoration, that which is too lofty — all that can be attained through perseverance, because perseverance is invincible and the mightiest resource).

— Chaanakya Neeti Darpanah: 7.3

How to Shape up Desire

When you desire something intensely, it becomes a passion that energises and fuels your potential. We know that complacent people lack zeal, enthusiasm and initiative because they do not yearn earnestly for anything more than what they consider most essential. Security concerns, not ambitions, seem to drive these people.

Alexander the Great, Babur and a host of other achievers, through the history, were young boys when they started giving shape to their dreams and desires. They conquered countries and continents because they had the urge to achieve, the desire to fulfill.

Your earnest yearning shows and you can't hide it. It dominates your thinking, your feelings, your relationships, conversations and actions. What distinguishes the human being from rest of the animal kingdom is his unique ability to conceive ideas about future, analyse these and reason out a choice of action. Behavioural scientists explain that impulse is transmitted through electro-chemical processes across the synapses — the tiny spaces less than one thousandth of a millimetre, which keep the neurons apart in the brain. When similar thoughts occur in the mind quite often, they form patterns. When identical ideas traverse this mental territory repeatedly, it becomes a habit. It is something akin to country-folks, and even cattle, moving across vast tracts of land every day. Even though they tread the area where there are no tracks, yet from their repeated movement, trails and tracks are formed. It is these trails and tracks that become pathways, roads and highways to carry civilisations through the ages to this day. As a contrast to this, stray thoughts, that only sometimes drift into and vanish from the mind, fail to establish a trail.

When your cherished ideas visit your mind quite frequently, a desire forms. When you entertain it, fondle it and play with it in your mind, it often changes from one shape to another, till it crystallises into a concrete form.

Now, when you are in a position to clearly visualise your dream, your desire, embellish it with more details and make a list of the same. For example, think of the scenario on fulfillment of this desire. What benefits will accrue to you, your family or your business? If you were to abandon it right here, what disadvantages are you likely to suffer? What difference can it make to you and your family in their lifestyle? Write down every point in a diary — it is important. In the process of writing, you will connect and proceed from one idea to another, each rejuvenating and intensifying your desire and resolve to formulate and achieve your goal.

WRITTEN STATEMENT OF GOAL

Thoughts in the mind are in abstract form. When you write them down on a piece of paper, the mechanical act of inscribing characters becomes a multi-faculty endeavour. Your mind thinks, your hand writes and your eyes watch. Thoughts remain shapeless until they come out of the mind. Writing clothes them and makes them clearly visible as distinct entities.

Besides, words trigger emotions and convey pictures. Try and say PUKE silently to yourself. How do you feel? Now say SPRINKLE? Your reactions are vastly different — not only in the mind, but physically, too. I often notice faces of people in the audience pucker up at the mention of the first word, while the mention of the latter smoothens the pucker on their foreheads. This is because words affect us more powerfully than raw, unexpressed thoughts. Almost always, a goal at the inception stage floats in the mind in the vague shape of *something*. When you express it in writing, it becomes more tangible. The words first tingle your conscious mind and then make a niche to stay in solid form in your mind.

A goal defined in written form is no longer a wandering thought. It is the product of your desire in its tangible dimensions. The written statement of your goal itself becomes your motivator now. The more you read it, the more it stirs up your imagination. Over a period of time, you might also like to modify and reframe your *statement of goal.* By all means do that. In fact, you can make it a weekly exercise for the first four weeks — write it and leave it until next weekend. Then again read it, reframe and restate it. This fine tuning will finally give you the goal as it should be for you.

While doing this exercise, be careful not to abandon the previously conceived goal altogether and begin to crave for new goals every time. That would be an antithesis of what I am recommending here. You should evolve and fine tune the product of your intense desires, yearnings. To ensure that you do not stray into alien territory, fix the core of your goal and let it remain the object of your focus. You can change everything else but do not disturb the core of your goal. So, whenever you re-write your goal, do not tear and throw away your previous notes. Preserve them and refer to them whenever you feel the need for a change, improvement or modification.

DEALING WITH OBSTACLES

If you think that once you have drawn up your plan, the road will lay itself out in front of you for a joyous, trouble-free journey, you will be surprised. The road ahead, like any other in real life, is a mix of smooth, rough and bumpy. There will be stretches with broken and pitted surface. There will be puddles and boggy patches too. There may be stretches passing through sandy terrain with no refuelling and service station for long distances. All these are necessary concomitants of the journey that every traveller has to go through. You do not find people abandoning their vehicle and wherewithal midway in wilderness. Continuous movement ahead, even if a little jerky, does take you to your destination. A little thought and vision will make you foresee the obstacles and prepare you better to cross the road. You will have to bypass and use diversions where the straight road is strewn with boulders, pits or other roadblocks. Most of these obstacles would have been visualised and planned for, if you had planned carefully as suggested earlier in this chapter.

Now how do you bypass roadblocks hindering the attainment of your goal? The most serious roadblocks that you must avoid and bypass from the beginning are people who either do not understand your goal or do not share your ideology about your cherished goal, because they are nothing but detractors. Also, think of any other circumstance that may be blocking the progress, review your plan and develop appropriate strategy to overcome or bypass the same. Prior visualisation helps in pre-planning a sound Action Plan to overcome these roadblocks, as and when you come across them.

GARNER EXTERNAL SUPPORT

It is fair to assume that you would need skills, people and material. You will perhaps need to educate and prepare yourself too. So, associate with people and organisations who can contribute in furthering your movement towards your goal. It would be a kind of an ongoing research and survey that will keep you in tune with the latest trends in the field of your activity. Get to know more people in the same field. Share your ideas with them and avail of their experience. When you listen to them you will know how they solved their problems which you might be facing now, and how they feel being at the top of their goal today. Their answers to such questions will boost your morale and show you a new beam of light too.

Internet is an infinite reservoir that has something for all your needs in the world today. Be it encyclopaedic information, specific subject research, expert advice, market intelligence, B2B transactions, e-commerce or any other industrial, social, professional, academic information — Internet has it all. It is a very quick and economical means of communication too. Make full use of it.

Insist on Deadlines

The more time people have, the more sluggish they become. Students never study as much throughout the year as they study in one month prior to the exams. Why? Because with a long rope, time does not seem to pull fast enough. A loose rope can pull nothing! Allocation of too much time also defeats the purpose. People work more efficiently when they have to function in a tight time-frame. Deadlines sharpen your thinking, narrow your focus on the requirement and establish urgency and importance, both together. Think of your likely reactions as Rahul, General Manager (Marketing) in a packaging company, to the requirements given to you:

Option 1: "Rahul, we need to expand our customer base. Let's discuss one of these days, when you have time. I would like to have your views on what can be done."

Option 2: "Rahul, we must expand our customer base by 20 per cent by March 2003. Please, plan your strategy and discuss it with me next Monday."

How do you feel about Option 1? Not urgent, nor anything specific. "Oh! Why do we need to expand our customer base?

I'll see if I have time one of these days....". But what about Option 2? It is urgent, specific and with a deadline. "Ah, expand by 20 per cent? By March 2003? And I'm to prepare and present a strategy by next Monday! I must get cracking..!"

Deadlines are actually lifelines for achieving success. Anything that does not have a deadline is most likely to linger on. Deadlines must be assigned to separate segments of your goal. Each segment or stage of progress towards the goal must have its own time-frame. Cumulatively all these deadlines should converge on the final deadline of overall accomplishment. It would be even more useful if the deadlines in the form of a check-list displayed are in your office/workplace, so as to remind you from time to time.

Deadlines can also create confusion if everything is required to be accomplished at one time. It is not possible, nor is it required. Things must move as per the time-plan in a graduated sequence; so prioritise your work. Each segment or stage of work must be allotted the priority it deserves. Faulty prioritisation can wreck the whole plan. Here is a story that explains the importance of allotting right priority to goals and activities in life:

A philosophy professor stood before his class with some items in front of him. When the class began, wordlessly he picked up a large empty mayonnaise jar and proceeded to fill it with rocks of about 2" in diameter. He then asked the students if the jar was full? They agreed that it was.

The professor then picked up a box of pebbles and poured them into the jar. He shook the jar lightly. The pebbles, of course, rolled into the open areas between the rocks. He then asked the students again if the jar was full. They agreed it was.

The students laughed. The professor picked up a box of sand and poured it into the jar. Of course, the sand filled up everything else.

"Now," said the professor, "I want you to recognise that this is your life. The rocks are the important things — your family, your partner, your health, your children — things, that if everything else were lost and only they remained, your life would still be full. The pebbles are the other things that matter — like your job, your house, your car. The sand is everything else. The small and minor stuff.

"If you put the sand into the jar first, there is no room for the pebbles or the rocks. The same goes for your life. If you spend all your time and energy on the small stuff, you will never have room for things that are important to you. Pay attention to the things that are critical to your happiness. Play with your children. Take time to get medical check-ups done. Take your partner out dancing. There will always be time to go to work, clean the house, give a dinner party and fix the disposal. Take care of the rocks first — the things that really matter. Set your priorities. The rest is just sand."

But then, a student then took the jar, which the other students and the professor agreed was full, and proceeded to pour in a glass of beer. Of course, the beer filled the remaining spaces within the jar, making the jar truly full.

The moral of this tale is: That no matter how full your life is, there is always room for BEER! Call it cheer!

See Success, Feel Success

Why are dreams so important? Daydreaming is the key to all big ideas. Those who do not build castles in the air cannot make concrete castles on solid ground either. Any idea becomes a reality in the outer world only once it has been conceived in the mind. Dreams are your periscope that transcend your present status and provide you a peep into the future.

The human brain has the incredible capacity to store an enormous amount of information from the past. Somebody mentions the name of your schoolfriend and the whole era of schooltime spreads in the mind vividly. Interestingly, while it stores every past experience of our existence, our brain does not need help from other parts of the body to look into the future of our desires. When we think of our goal, we do have a vision of the likely future. Now, imagine the future of your visualisation has been reached. How do you feel being at the top of your goal? A successful person you always wanted to be! Visualise its impact on your family, friends, relatives and society around you. When you are in a position to transcend beyond immediate moments into the distant future in such visualisation, you are seeing the colour of success. Close your eyes for a while and taste it. How are you feeling being different from what you were when you had not even started for this goal? It will arouse healthy, vibrant sensations in you. Enjoy it. Whatever goes on in our minds immensely influences our actions and their outcome in real life. Do this future imaging often and you will find that you have more energy, vision and proper orientation in the pursuit of your goal.

Ashmanvati reeyate sam rabhdhvamuttishthat
pra tarataa sakhaayah.
Atraa jahaam ye asannashevaah ye
shivaanvayamuttaremaabhi vaajaan.

(This world is a white water river, meandering through rocks and boulders. Friends! Rise, dare and accomplish your voyage. Relinquish all that is a source of sorrow and misery. Rise and espouse a goal that will bring you happiness and glory).

—Rig Veda: 10.53.8

Focus 7: Dream and See Your Goal Fructify

- You must dream — as you must have in the past too — to 'achieve' in life. Write down these ideas in a diary. Revise and update these periodically. Ideas are like seeds; water them regularly. They will sprout into plans and bloom into real future!
- Look far ahead. Don't fall prey to narrow, short-term gains and temptations.
- Carry forward 'lessons' of the past; not 'sorrows'. Apply these lessons to purge your today's pursuits and prepare with full zeal to receive your future with laurels!
- Time is more precious than money. But it is equitably distributed to all without discrimination. Manage it well and make full use of it through strict self-discipline.
- Enrich your abilities and self-confidence through regular preparation and constant belief in your own potential. Auto-suggestions are of great value in enhancing one's abilities and faith within for a better performance. Tell yourself: 'I can learn it soon', 'I have the requisite energy and will power to achieve it', etc.
- Everyone has his/her own vision and goals in life. A review of your goals in the light of this focus may result in some additional short-term goals. Now, take stock of four things: your goals, your abilities, resources (required vis-à-vis available) and time (i.e. the

(Contd.)

deadline you set for yourself). Review your goals and update them from time to time.

- Allot priorities to your goals and prepare a self-check for self-accountability to ensure that appropriate attention, effort, time and resources are being given for attainment of each of the goals as per their priority.
- 'Knowledge is power'. Make self-education a routine and regular habit. Gain in-depth knowledge of your job; working knowledge of systems and happenings around you; and a fair amount of your mission. Monitor regular progress.
- Commit yourself to a mission, i.e. the attainment of your goal. Study and analyse inputs to add impetus to your mission. Monitor regular progress.
- Competition is a great source of energy, ideas and inspiration. Welcome it and face it competently. If you don't have competition, you do not know whether you are moving or not. Seek competition and you will be on your way to 'excellence'.

SPECIFIC ACTION PLAN

A - How would you like your life to be, like say, ten years from now? Concretise your dreams into specific goals. Specify these goals here.

a) ______________________________

____

b) ______________________________

____

c) ______________________________

____

B - Now choose one goal out of the aforesaid goals that is most important to you. State it clearly here (remember it must be precise and time-bound).

____

C - You cannot do a goal; you can do an action. And it is through actions that you reach your goal. So now, make a list of all the things/actions you will have to do to achieve that goal.

a)

b)

c)

d)

e)

f)

g)

D - Identify and mention here the names of those achievers with whom you would like to associate and discuss your plans.

E - List out the specific tasks and their priorities as decided by you in respect of your goal.